SIMON N. LEONARD
SAMUEL FOWLER
JOHNPAUL KENNEDY
DEBORAH DEVIS

PRAGMATIC ADAPTIVE LEADERSHIP

Tools for Guiding in Complex Educational Systems

POLICY PRESS SHORTS RESEARCH

First published in Great Britain in 2025 by

Policy Press, an imprint of
Bristol University Press
University of Bristol
1–9 Old Park Hill
Bristol
BS2 8BB
UK
t: +44 (0)117 374 6645
e: bup-info@bristol.ac.uk

Details of international sales and distribution partners are available at
policy.bristoluniversitypress.co.uk

© Simon N. Leonard, Samuel Fowler, JohnPaul Kennedy and Deborah Devis 2025

The digital PDF and ePub versions of this title are available open access and distributed
under the terms of the Creative Commons Attribution-NonCommercial-NoDerivatives 4.0
International licence (https://creativecommons.org/licenses/by-nc-nd/4.0/) which permits
reproduction and distribution for non-commercial use without further permission provided the
original work is attributed.

British Library Cataloguing in Publication Data
A catalogue record for this book is available from the British Library

ISBN 978-1-4473-7697-2 paperback
ISBN 978-1-4473-7698-9 ePub
ISBN 978-1-4473-7699-6 ePdf

The right of Simon N. Leonard, Samuel Fowler, JohnPaul Kennedy and Deborah Devis
to be identified as authors of this work has been asserted by them in accordance with the
Copyright, Designs and Patents Act 1988.

All rights reserved: no part of this publication may be reproduced, stored in a retrieval system,
or transmitted in any form or by any means, electronic, mechanical, photocopying, recording,
or otherwise without the prior permission of Bristol University Press.

Every reasonable effort has been made to obtain permission to reproduce copyrighted material.
If, however, anyone knows of an oversight, please contact the publisher.

The statements and opinions contained within this publication are solely those of the authors
and not of the University of Bristol or Bristol University Press. The University of Bristol
and Bristol University Press disclaim responsibility for any injury to persons or
property resulting from any material published in this publication.

Bristol University Press and Policy Press work to counter discrimination on
grounds of gender, race, disability, age and sexuality.

Cover design: Chris Wilson
Front cover image: iStock/Vertigo3d
Bristol University Press and Policy Press use environmentally
responsible print partners.
Printed and bound in Great Britain by CPI Group (UK) Ltd,
Croydon, CR0 4YY

Bristol University Press' authorised representative in the
European Union is: Easy Access System Europe,
Mustamäe tee 50, 10621 Tallinn, Estonia,
Email: gpsr.requests@easproject.com

Contents

List of figures and tables		iv
About the authors		vi
Acknowledgements		viii
one	Navigating the complexity of schooling	1
two	Future-oriented decision making	17
three	Future-oriented learning	39
four	The complexity of learning contexts	63
five	Pragmatic Adaptive Modelling: expanding the educational world	95
six	Pragmatic Adaptive Leadership: building the supports for self-regulated learning	123
Glossary		148
References		155
Index		173

List of figures and tables

Figures
1.1	Three kinds of leadership	7
1.2	Practices of Pragmatic Adaptive Leadership	10
1.3	Tension in an activity system	14
3.1	A black box view of the mass education process	41
3.2	A representation of the Organization for Economic Co-operation and Development's transformative competencies framework	47
3.3	The elements of an activity system	51
3.4	A representation of the self-regulated learning system	56
4.1	Observed teacher and student practices during a 3D modelling learning activity	71
4.2	A systems representation of a hypothetical science learning system and four simultaneous activity systems, some with unique objects of transformation, others with shared objects of transformation	74
4.3	A black box process representation of the sheep shearing activity	80
4.4	Sheep shearing theory of change	81
4.5	Woollen products assumptions and risks	82
4.6	Situational map of sheep shearing activity	84
4.7	Enablers of sheep shearing activity	87
4.8	Tensions in sheep shearing activity	89
4.9	Tensions between the parallel activities of sheep shearing and crop management on Old MacDonald's farm	92
5.1	Traditional view of a learning activity system	99
5.2	School Attitudes Survey hotspot map for Winnie	102
5.3	A cross-cohort look at School Attitudes Survey data for Winnie's peers at Corroboree Frog College*	103
5.4	A sample of some Wellbeing and Engagement Collection trends across time	106

5.5	Some Wellbeing and Engagement Collection trends across time as seen at Corroboree Frog College and the typical development of these factors by school year	108
5.6	Modelling a student's simultaneous activity systems and future trajectory	109
5.7	Tensions in a student's activity system that may affect long-term outcomes	112
5.8	Impact of teaching activity on student activity	117
5.9	Modelling across complex systems	118
5.10	Professional learning activity system	119
6.1	Linked systems involved in developing self-regulated learning	127
6.2	Teacher and leader activity supports student activity	128
6.3	Intersystem tensions in SRL activities	131
6.4	Research-Informed Design template	134
6.5	Design evaluation protocol	139

Tables

1.1	The practices, principles and protocols of Pragmatic Adaptive Leadership	12
3.1	Mapping of framework elements to activity system objects	52

*A larger and more dynamic representation of the data in Figure 5.3 is available online at https://bristoluniversitypress.co.uk/pragmatic-adaptive-leadership

About the authors

Deborah Devis is Research Fellow at Adelaide University. Deborah's research focus is on knowledge brokerage, activity theory and systems thinking for educational change. She currently leads an educational design team focused on practical, co-designed solutions to complex educational problems. Deborah has held roles as a knowledge broker, researcher and communicator across multiple industries, including education, science, journalism and the arts.

Samuel Fowler is Lecturer in Education at Adelaide University. Samuel's research examines the implicit psychological aspects of learning – such as epistemic beliefs, metacognition, motivation and self-regulated learning – and explores how this understanding can inform the development of meaningful, authentic learning experiences for both teachers and students. With extensive classroom teaching experience, he collaborates with schools and education systems to strengthen teachers' pedagogical reasoning and address the complexities of holistic teaching.

JohnPaul Kennedy is Senior Lecturer in Education at Adelaide University. Informed by 15 years in the school classroom, his research sits at the nexus of educational theory and practice. JohnPaul's research is centred around understanding students' attitudes towards schooling and the effect these have on student learning outcomes. He currently leads an educational data team that is focused on developing lightweight measurement instruments that can be used to gain rapid insights into complex education systems to facilitate data-informed change for schools.

Simon N. Leonard is Professor of the Learning Sciences at Adelaide University. Simon's research focus is on understanding and guiding complex activities like learning and leadership within complex contexts like schools. As a practitioner-researcher, he currently leads his university's equity and participation partnerships with schools and programmes developing new pathways to teaching and school leadership. Simon has previously held a range of educational leadership roles in both schools and universities.

Acknowledgements

This book – and the work it represents – has only been possible through the long-standing support of our learning partners at 'Corroboree Frog College'. We are at once in awe of the professionalism and ethics of care we find in that place, and appreciative of the willingness of this community to engage with our research team, right from its beginning. Thanks particularly to Nick for your vision of leadership, and to Wayne and Lesley for your tireless work spanning the boundaries between our organisations.

Our thanks go also to our team at the Education Futures Academy Team. The graphic design of Tia Le Cerf has greatly improved our capacity to communicate complex ideas in this book and elsewhere. Our research assistants, Maesie MacGillivray, Nicole Vass, Ashley Platt and Lisa Smith, have helped us work through the diverse data sets we have used to test the approaches reported in this book. Kim Giannoni has coordinated our ever-growing list of school partnerships and ensured effective liaison back into the complex organisation that is our own institution. While Joe Matthews and Andrew Tuovinen have assisted with website design, proofreading and many other tasks. And to the rest of the team, we thank you for your contributions to the creation of such a wonderful place to engage in teaching and research.

ONE

Navigating the complexity of schooling

School education is a complex enterprise. In saying this, we are not talking about the logistical challenges of organising a school. Coordinating timetables and resources and all that goes on in a busy school day is certainly *complicated*, but there are stable solutions to those challenges. The *complexity* we are talking about here is a more intrinsic feature of supporting the learning and development of young people. To simultaneously engage in young people's cognitive, social, emotional and even spiritual development; to pay attention to their health and wellbeing; and to ensure that they are able to participate in their community, their society and the political economy. Now *that* is complex, however it is organised.

This book is about leadership in the midst of this complexity. Importantly, it is also about leadership in an era when it is increasingly recognised that the ways in which schools have been governed and led have left our schools less rather than more able to meet the future challenges our educational enterprise will face (Lupton and Hayes, 2021). Instead, there is tendency towards market-based, capitalist solutions, where knowledge is seen as a commodity and students as consumers – a type of thinking called 'neoliberalism'. Neoliberal thinking is essentially based on the idea that the market should decide, and this tends to require the development of proxies for the 'price signal' of a natural market. Much has been written about the rise in neoliberal ideas that have shaped education policies, leadership and governance over the past few decades (see, for example, Connell, 2013; Tett and Hamilton, 2019), and how these ideas came to have such influence (Mirowski and Plehwe, 2015). This book will not add much to this already substantial critique. Rather, our focus will be on what school leaders, teachers and others within a school community can do within schools as they exist, within an ongoing neoliberal atmosphere.

Let us quickly introduce our context. This book on leadership is written by a group of researchers whose work is in the Learning Sciences. That is, our expertise lies in the study of learning situated in visible practice. You will not be surprised, then, to know that our interest in leadership is in relation to how it supports learning and development. Although this is our focus, we do not discount the need for leadership around other functions within schools, such as human resources, facilities management and so on. It is just that our expertise is in learning, and, particularly, in translating and enacting educational research into 'real world' settings. This book is one of the ways we seek to support the enactment work we do.

For leadership to be effective in the ongoing chaos of a school, it must be pragmatic and adaptive in response to change. We will share our approach to this leadership – which we call *Pragmatic Adaptive Leadership (PAL)* – throughout this book. This approach shares an evolutionary history with many other alternatives that have been proposed for educational leadership over recent decades and uses elements of many common models. For readers with a deeper interest in theory (and jargon), PAL is essentially the result of bringing together the *Expansive Learning Theory* of Engeström (1987), the *Complexity Leadership Theory* (CLT) of Uhl-Bien et al (2007), and some of the ideas from programme evaluation like *Contribution Analysis* (Mayne, 2008) and *Developmental Evaluation* (Patton, 2011). In putting these theoretical positions in conversation, we hope that the book makes a useful contribution to an ongoing discussion and debate in the literature around the need for and shape of a fourth generation of Activity Theory (also known as Cultural Historical Activity Theory; Spinuzzi and Guile, 2019; Engeström and Sannino, 2021).

But, putting all that jargon aside, we know that the everyday changemakers of education don't necessarily have the time to dive deeply into theory in the same way researchers do. Bearing this in mind, we have made every endeavour to ensure the book is also accessible to readers with less interest in theory, but who want to make better use of the knowledge generated by educational research when shaping what goes on in their school. After all, if we are being 'pragmatic' – like it says in the title – accessibility is the key to good research translation. As enactment is a major focus of our research, we hope this book will be most useful in the hands of teachers and school leaders who are working to drive evidence-informed and future-oriented change. We are seeking to translate the theoretical frameworks we use in our own research in the Learning Sciences into a set of practices and protocols that can help guide change within the complex systems and contexts in which schools operate.

PAL is explicitly a theory of research translation. It is intended to assist schools and school leaders in making the best use of the full diversity of educational research – particularly research in the *Science of Learning and Development* (Darling-Hammond et al, 2020) – to inform, scale and sustain effective innovation. With this purpose of translation in mind, PAL is deeply future-oriented. It is concerned with continuously adapting our systems of teaching and learning in response to the never-ending flow of new knowledge from research and professional practice.

In our own collaborative research work, which we will use to illustrate our arguments throughout the book, this search for 'next' practice has tended to settle on the idea of student and teacher agency, motivation and self-regulation.

This is because this cluster of ideas has been appearing at the leading edge of research and policy in recent years. However, we also recognise that priorities and needs change over time, so this book should be read with a focus on the *process* of change, regardless of the content. The practices and protocols we introduce should be transferable to different areas of professional focus.

This is a short book intended to introduce PAL as a way of working in and with schools, and the book is structured to reflect the way we work when using the PAL model ourselves. In Chapters Three to Six, we will tell the story of using PAL in a school we refer to by the pseudonym 'Corroboree Frog College' (CFC), with whom we have had a long-term relationship. Chapter Two is a little different. It contains an essay that connects our work to wider debates on education and educational governance. It too, though, is an example of the PAL way of working as it offers a form of *Futures Thinking*.

In and among our 'worked examples', the book will also provide a more explicit account of our Theory of Pragmatic Leadership. We'll begin that task now by clarifying what we mean by 'complexity' and 'leadership'.

Complexity

PAL uses the term 'complexity' as it is used in complexity science. Complexity science does not provide us with a unified theory or definition of complexity. Ironically, perhaps, it remains a complex space. In essence, though, complex systems are understood to involve a collection of elements that interact dynamically and non-linearly. They have multiple feedback loops that both drive and prevent change, they can function under conditions far from equilibrium, and they exhibit self-organisation and 'emergence' (Woolcott et al, 2021). In simpler terms, complex systems are more than the sum of their parts because they have behaviours that can't be explained by their parts alone.

Some classic complex systems include the brain, where intelligence 'emerges' from the complex interactions of millions of neurons; and ecosystems, where the introduction of a new species can have large, non-linear and often completely unexpected effects on the way the system operates. Some systems have predictable behaviour, like a solar system or computer program. Others lead to unpredictable behaviour, like a weather system causing a heatwave in winter, or a baking competition that devolves into a food fight. Education systems are the latter; unpredictable, changeable and prone to emergence.

We do not have to think too hard to see complexity working in learning and development. Take something as simple as reading instruction. We often hear discussion of reading instruction as though it is a simple, linear system – apply 'pedagogy X' and reading skill will improve. But 'reading' is complex, it is about more than decoding words. Reading is also about comprehension, motivation, interest, purpose, emotional reactions and even identity. In other words, a strategy focused on developing the decoding skill won't necessarily make a better 'reader', just a better 'decoder'. Such a strategy may even have the opposite effect if, say, it increases a young person's anxiety when asked to read, or destroys their love of reading all together! Such interactions are part of the complexity we are dealing with here. It is the complexity of everyday teaching and learning.

Of course, school systems and educational policy demands add to the inherent complexity of learning and development. For example, students are often asked to navigate the cognitive and motivational complexity of deep thinking but are also constrained by rigid school timetables beyond their control. What happens if a student is deep in thought when the bell rings for the end of class, or if they are distracted pondering an idea from two lessons ago? Similarly, we ask teachers to support their students to be intellectual risk takers, but they all still exist within a system that demands high-stakes exams as a measure of overall 'success'. How do they decide when it is too risky to be a risk taker? The work of schooling for both teachers and students is *always* about balancing competing priorities and resolving tensions. It is work that always takes place within the cognitive, emotional and social entanglements of human life. And that is always complex.

While we aim for pragmatism, we also recognise that PAL must be complex enough to engage with these everyday complexities. We'll endeavour to make it as user-friendly as possible, but we do so recognising that complexity theory tells us that complex systems can only be guided by a complex response (Boisot and McKelvey, 2011).

Leadership

PAL's approach to leadership draws on concepts from complexity science – specifically, the CLT of Uhl-Bien et al (2007). In proposing CLT, Uhl-Bien and colleagues argued that we should recognise three broad types of leadership. First, they said, there is *administrative leadership*. This is the traditional, hierarchical, 'top-down' leadership that first comes to mind at the mention of leadership. It is the type of leadership that is 'baked in' to the bureaucratic structure of most schools with their principals and heads of 'this and that'.

But CLT has two other ideas of leadership: adaptive and enabling leadership. To understand these, we first need to separate the idea of *leadership* from the idea of *leaders*. *Adaptive leadership* is understood primarily as a dynamic that exists in the interactions between agents and outcomes, in a specific context. It is 'bottom-up', creative and emergent, and it does not sit with or within any one person. Instead of describing a person, it describes a behaviour. *Enabling leadership*, on the other hand, tends to sit with middle managers, who have access to resources and can use their direct involvement to enable the conditions in which adaptive leadership is possible. Enabling leaders also play the key roles of distributing innovations of adaptive leadership, and of working at the boundary between systems.

In our own work, and within PAL, we are not advocating for one of these forms of leadership over another. Rather, we would argue that all are needed within the school context and that all three concepts of leadership are likely to co-exist in any given institution. We consider them not as points on a one-dimensional scale from top-down to bottom-up, but rather as shown in Figure 1.1, as the vertices of a plane. Thus, at any particular time, different groups of agents within the organisation are likely to be at different places on this plane, be experiencing different dynamics and perceiving problems or needs from different vantage points. That said, it is evident that schools do administrative leadership well, on the whole. But in this book we are concerned with enabling adaptive leadership while also ensuring we do not slip out into chaos (Stacey, 2007).

Figure 1.1: Three kinds of leadership

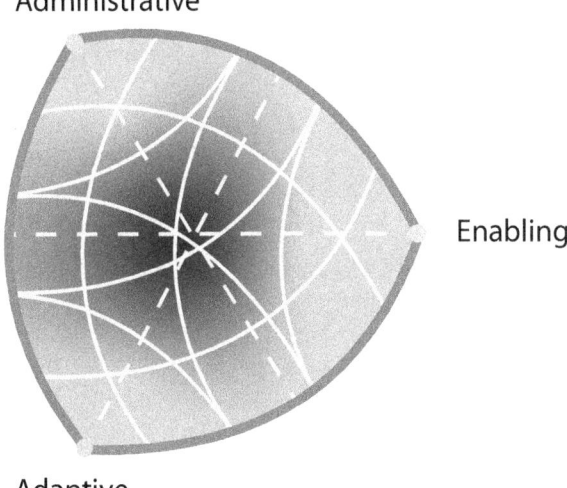

Ultimately, this book is about navigating the entanglements that we find in schools between administrative bureaucracy and adaptive, post-bureaucratic demands. The book offers a set of theory-informed and research-tested *practices* that support the emergence of adaptive, innovative action in schools, while still allowing the school, its staff, students and community to traverse the social and political contexts in which they are situated.

A Theory of Pragmatic Adaptive Leadership

Models for leadership and organisational change are often discussed in terms of being 'top-down' or 'bottom-up'. The CLT model we discussed earlier, for example, essentially seeks to balance the top-down of the traditional hierarchy with the bottom-up potential of creative emergence. In our own work at the interface of educational research and practice, however, a real challenge we have found in achieving this balance is that schools have many things pushing in 'horizontally'. That is to say, schools are always engaged with multiple – and often competing – agendas, and they interact with stakeholder groups that can make competing demands.

Even interactions with government-as-funder alone, for example, are quite complex. One policy initiative may focus on basic skills. Another – possibly from the same department – may focus on wellbeing, or the development of social skills. A different government department may drive the development of work-ready industry skills, or possibly transferable capabilities. Another department still may prioritise something like civics and citizenship, or the shaping of a national identity and set of values. A school must navigate *all* these demands at once, and that isn't even considering other external stakeholders. Schools are also engaged with the expectations of parents, media commentary, industry and social groups, and even the students themselves. And somewhere in all of that we also ask schools, teachers and students to respond to educational researchers like us. All these voices are telling schools to do different things, and that can shift leadership one way or the other.

PAL diverges from models like CLT and Expansive Learning Theory by addressing this web of horizontal influences, aligning with Engeström's call to develop a 'theoretically ambitious and empirically rigorous interventionist methodology for the learning sciences' (Engeström and Sannino, 2010; Sannino et al, 2016) and a move towards a fourth generation of Activity Theory. In short, PAL recognises that these voices exist and that we can work within them. It is about finding ways to act within a context that has interconnected activities occurring in parallel, all at once. We propose that the horizontal nature of PAL is what makes it so valuable in helping *enable* the *adaptive* possibilities to emerge from educational research, while still addressing the *administrative* demands of neoliberal governance.

To set this out more fully, our Theory of Pragmatic Adaptive Leadership is as follows. Learning and development within our educational institutions typically involves an entanglement of administrative and adaptive activities. However, the object and arrangements of each activity are sometimes invisible to people who are otherwise engaged. To enable and guide change within this mosaic of activity, we must first make these activities visible so we can comprehend them. But we also know that systems can have unpredictable emergent behaviours, so while we argue that leading transformative change requires the creation of visible, testable and shareable models, they cannot be fixed. We must be adaptable when change inevitably comes. In keeping with the pragmatic ethos, the validity of a PAL model is contingent on whether it 'works' in a given context – and when the model fails, it should be updated through empirical evidence.

The practices of Pragmatic Adaptive Leadership

In order to make the Theory of PAL more concrete, we highlight the kinds of *practices* it promotes. These practices do not require a deep engagement with the scholarly literature to orchestrate change, but it can be useful to understand the purpose or 'principle' behind each of the practices.

The *PAL practices* we will work though in this book are set out in Figure 1.2 and, more fully, in Table 1.1. These practices are not used sequentially, nor as part of a cycle, which reflects their use in engaging with complex systems. Rather, they are a collection of practices that we have found useful in our own school collaborations in response to what is occurring within a given project, and they can be moved as the project demands. Three of the practices – Futures Thinking, Situation Mapping and Futures Modelling – we collectively refer to as Pragmatic Adaptive Modelling (PAM). The other three – Design Thinking, Research-Informed Design and Reflexive Practice – we frequently combine under the heading of

Figure 1.2: Practices of Pragmatic Adaptive Leadership

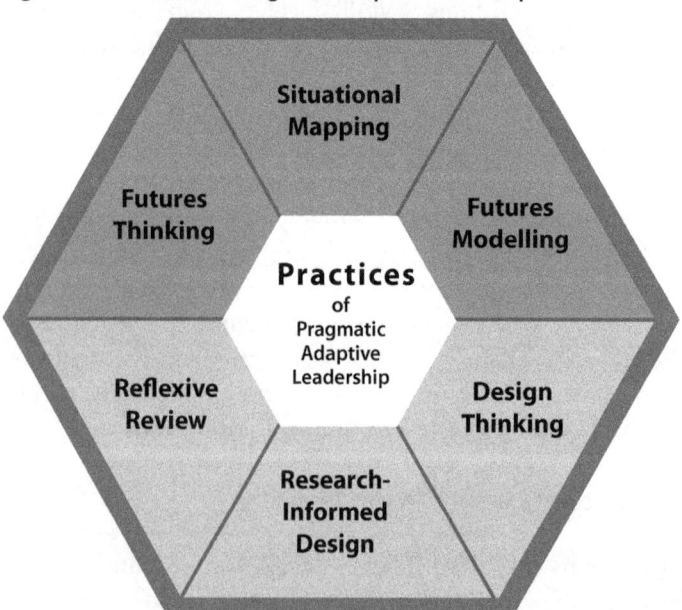

Pragmatic Adaptive Design. Within each practice, we also make use of a range of *protocols*, only some of which are covered in this book. Protocols are essentially the 'how to' guides on enacting a particular practice.

Futures Thinking

While not implemented in order, the practices are perhaps easiest to understand in the sequence we have listed them in Table 1.1. *Futures Thinking* (Canina et al, 2020) is an idea that has gained a lot of attention in the policy and consultancy world. It is usually understood as a strategic approach to critically considering future scenarios in order to define a preferred path forward. We are most interested in the essential disposition of Futures Thinking as being *divergent*. The entire point of the practice – what we refer to as the principle behind the practice – is not to predict the future, but rather to provide participants with ways to cope with uncertainty and complexity. That is, the practice allows participants to uncover multiple potential futures and thus consider ways in which they might choose, or need, to respond in each case. In our use we see the divergent character of Futures Thinking as a useful way to bridge gaps between parallel activity systems we find in everyday schools. The protocols we use to enact this practice include the humble essay as included in Chapter Two of this book, the participatory foresight methodology (UNDP Global Centre for Public Service Excellence, 2018), and our own *Hybrid Local Learning Hubs*.

Situational Mapping

Situational Mapping is a name we draw from third generation *Activity Theory* (3GAT), and the protocol we have frequently used to enact it is from the excellent manual on conducting Activity Systems Analysis provided by Yamagata-Lynch (2010). Sandoval's (2014) 'conjecture mapping' is similarly a useful protocol. Activity Theory essentially invites us to model how

Table 1.1: The practices, principles and protocols of Pragmatic Adaptive Leadership

Practice	Principle	Protocols
Futures Thinking	Scaffold participants to cope with uncertainty	• Essay • Hybrid Local Learning Hubs
Situational Mapping	Highlight the complexity (non-linearity) of the contexts schools work in and with	• Activity Systems Analysis • Conjecture mapping
Futures Modelling	Make the desired change visible and 'testable' while allowing for the complex	• Contribution analysis • Macro-system analysis
Design Thinking	Gain agreement on how to translate models into pragmatic action in school setting	• Journey mapping • Rapid concept development/prototyping • Student co-creation
Research-Informed Design	Use the principles gleaned from the relevant research to design educational activity, resources and environments that lead towards the desired futures	• Delineate desired results • Development of design standards
Reflexive Review	Engage with a diversity of empirical evidence to determine if the model is 'working'. If not, then adapt the design or adapt the model	• Collaborative conferencing • Review against design standards • Evaluate theory of change

the thing we are changing in an activity – the 'object' – is being transformed and influenced by the tools and people enacting the change, as well as the social norms and divisions of labour that influence choice and action.

As a simple example, we might look at the activity of learning fractions. The object of transformation in this case is the students' conceptual understanding of fractions. The tools used in the activity might be pedagogical strategies, mathematics resources and fraction exercises. Often, these are the only two parts of activity that are considered, but the reality is that these activities take place in a cultural and historical context that guide how the activity proceeds. An example of a 'norm' that could affect this activity's outcome are the traditions and beliefs about how mathematics is learned. When these norms and system elements don't align, we call this a 'tension' or a contradiction.

In our fraction example, a common tension is created when traditional forms of teaching mathematics trigger academic emotions such as anxiety or boredom, and hence avoidance, in the student. Regardless of the tools, there is a contradiction between the social norm of traditional teaching methods, and the personal experiences of the student. In this case, we can see that the reason a student may not be learning their fractions has nothing to do with the tools used, but the underlying cause is invisible and social. This model is provided diagrammatically in Figure 1.3. In our practice, we use *Situational Mapping* to highlight the complexity of the system that we are working with to find both its limitations and its potentials.

Futures Modelling

Our approach to Situational Mapping differs from much of the research using 3GAT in that we have a strong interest in modelling what we have described earlier as the 'horizontal' pressures on an activity system as well as the internal tensions within it. In 3GAT analysis, there has been an assumption that the system will 'expand' outwards and transform largely due to internal tensions (Engeström, 1987), but we argue that in schools, external tensions are just as important. While we are interested in an expansive approach to the learning system, the tensions this system experiences frequently come from outside the activity system of the instructional practice of the classroom. This has led us to develop an additional practice

Figure 1.3: Tension in an activity system

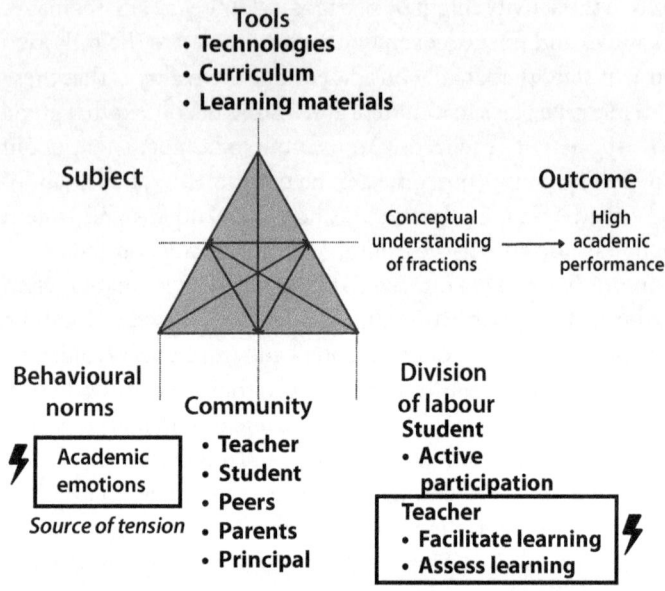

we refer to as *Futures Modelling*. This practice is novel in and of itself and will occupy a great deal of our attention in the later chapters of this book.

The principle behind this practice is that in a neoliberal context, there is a need to make the direction of change *visible* and *testable*. That is, our continued interaction with the existing bureaucratic infrastructure of our context means that we still need to be able to provide some form of *simple* measure to evaluate the effectiveness of an intervention. Futures Modelling is intended to achieve this level of visibility but does so without reducing our complex systems to a simple, linear equation.

Design Thinking and Research-Informed Design

As researchers from the Learning Sciences, Design-Based Research (DBR, also known as Educational Design Research;

McKenney and Reeves, 2013) is very much our 'home territory', and we have previously argued that it is a useful structure for change in schools (see, for example, Fowler and Leonard, 2021). As our work has evolved, however, we have found a need to strengthen the design practices of our professional partners in schools. While we imagine DBR as a 'conversation' between educational design professionals and educational researchers, we have found that in many DBR projects the researcher is, or is required by circumstances to become, the designer (Fowler et al, 2022a). With this in mind, we add the practices of *Design Thinking* and *Research-Informed Design* to our PAL practices. The principle behind each of these practices is that driving change across multiple dimensions of activity requires the development of careful and systematic design practice.

Reflexive Review

The ideas of reflecting on what we have been doing is not new to teachers. Reflection, taking the time to stop and consciously think about what we have been doing and experiencing and what we have learned from doing so, is now a quite standard pedagogy. The main thing we will say in introducing it as a PAL practice is that *Reflexive Review* should always be a deeply empirical practice. However, it should also look and feel very different to dominant forms of evaluation in the neoliberal governance of schools. Instead of reducing evaluation down to simple, marketable metrics, a *Reflexive Review* should reflect the complexity of the model building and design that has taken place in the other PAL practices, and it should account for the diverse entanglement of lived activity.

Enabling Pragmatic Adaptive Leadership

In this chapter we have introduced some of the basic ideas we'll be working with throughout the rest of the book. We've introduced some of them quite formally and offered what might be seen as scholarly definitions, and we've introduced some of them as practices that leaders and teachers in schools might adopt. In most of the chapters that follow, we'll seek to make these practices more concrete. We'll do this by describing how we have developed them and how we make use of them in our own work, and particularly in the work we have undertaken over many years with the school we call CFC.

In Chapter Three, we will introduce the overarching 'leadership' challenge that has been central to our engagement with CFC. It is a challenge we call the 'thriving after school' challenge in which the school has sought to do more than ensure its students do well at the 'game' of school. In introducing this challenge, we'll begin to describe how we have gone about some of the practices of PAM, and briefly look into some of the key research that has informed our work around this challenge. In Chapters Four and Five we will explore the practices of PAM further. In doing so we will discuss some of the theory underlying the PAM approach in greater detail than we have in this introduction, and we will explain our own innovations in modelling in complex contexts. In the final chapter, Chapter Six, we'll present what is essentially a work in progress and examine how we are continuing to work with CFC as their work shifts to a stronger Pragmatic Adaptive Design focus. In this context, we will give consideration to directions for further research in areas such as the way metrics and learning analytics might work with PAL, and how PAL can be used to improve equity outcomes in education.

As we have mentioned earlier, Chapter Two is a little different to the more practically oriented material that follows. In Chapter Two we offer an essay that situates our methodological design work within the broader context of the debates around educational leadership and governance. Those looking for something closer to a 'how to' guide might want to skip directly to Chapter Three, but for those wanting to think about some of the 'why' questions of educational leadership, read on in order.

TWO

Future-oriented decision making

This chapter was originally written as one of our *Futures Thinking* protocols – in this case, the protocol was simply an essay. This essay was written by one of us (Leonard) and was intended to serve as a catalyst for Futures Thinking within our own research team as we started to engage with schools in projects around issues like agency, anxiety and engagement. These are all issues that most stakeholders in a school will agree are important, but in the neoliberal context of school rankings based on high stakes testing results and the like, they are easily sidelined from the central decision-making processes of a school. As such, we needed to really think about our own processes because going out to schools with great advice drawn from the research could be completely ineffective if there are other stakeholder pressures that outcompete the advice.

As a protocol for doing this kind of deep thinking, the essay is an interesting option. The essay format has a long history entirely because it provides an organised and efficient way of exploring and understanding a set of interrelated ideas. These understandings are vital in the way we operate as an interdisciplinary team as the essay allows for all the pieces to be put in place in a way that is not possible in, say, a meeting. In saying this, we do recognise that teachers and school leaders rarely have the time and space in their professional lives to produce long essays. Nevertheless, we commend the essay as a pragmatic protocol for Futures Thinking in a school, although you may choose a more concise format than what follows in this chapter.

We share this essay now with a wider readership as it provides a solid introduction to the kinds of 'horizontal pressures' that have impacted the school sites we work with, and the kinds of scholarship that have guided our development of Pragmatic Adaptive Leadership as a means to lead meaningful action. The major purpose of this essay was, and is, to help us look beyond the assumptions and logics of our own context, and to reposition those assumptions as one choice among many.

From critique to an alternative infrastructure

Neoliberalism (Connell, 2013), and particularly its enactment through the cognitive and policy infrastructures of *New Public Management* (NPM; Hood, 1991), has been highly resilient to crisis. Not even a global financial crisis or a global pandemic have challenged its hegemonic dominance in public policy making – at least, in the Anglosphere. It has also been highly resilient to our critical scholarship of educational policy and practice. The critique of the current wave of neoliberal educational reform got underway over two decades ago now (see, for example, Gordon and Whitty, 1997; Karsten, 1999; Gorostiaga Derqui, 2001). Since then, indexes such as Scopus show that publications on the topic are growing exponentially. The search terms 'neoliberal' AND 'education' show the number of papers increasing year-on-year for the last 20 years. In 2022 the number has grown to no fewer than 632. This suggests there is a lot of scholarly work going on – a lot of effort by a lot of very clever and dedicated people. The continued growth of the genre, however, speaks loudly to its own lack of impact beyond the bibliographic metrics. In short, if our critique were hitting its mark, then there would be nothing left to write about.

Indeed, it is possible that this scholarship is actually counterproductive. Rowlands and Rawolle (2013) highlighted this a decade ago using the Bourdieuian concept of *illusio*. To Bourdieu and Wacquant (1992), *illusio* is what keeps the participants in a given 'field' – in our case, the field of education – playing the same 'game'. The collusion to play the same game, Bourdieu argued, is endorsed and sustained by a kind of fetishism. The practices, actions and capitals of a field have value only inasmuch as they are accepted by the field (Bourdieu, 1996). Rowlands and Rawolle did not go so far as to say that we have fetishised neoliberalism within the pages of our journals. They did argue, though, that the tendency to use 'neoliberal' as an imprecise concept tended to make it appear a 'theory of everything' and, hence, to contribute to the *illusio* that legitimises and sustains neoliberalism as the only 'game' we play in the field of education.

In this essay, I am seeking to sketch out the foundations of an alternative strategy for a pragmatic, adaptive educational policy making and leadership that is able to counter the ongoing violence that neoliberalism and the NPM are doing (Lohmeyer and Taylor, 2021). In doing so, I am seeking to continue the discussion begun by Rowlands and Rawolle (2013) that has continued in places including a special issue of *Discourse* (Rowe et al, 2019), but which I suggest ought be more prominent in our field.

To extend Bourdieu's 'game' metaphor, I am seeking to sketch out a strategy that does not seek to 'win' the 'neoliberal game', but instead seeks to de-centre neoliberalism, and to play a different game entirely. In seeking to avoid the traps of the neoliberal *illusio*, this essay will first highlight a very specific shortcoming of the neoliberal solution to governance that is the NPM. I will argue that NPM is inadequate in that it erroneously writes a complex world as simple. I will take particular issue with the use of proxies for 'price' that have been used, attempting to solve what Hayek (1945) framed as the 'knowledge problem' of classical Weberian bureaucracy, and with the modes of knowledge production that this approach valorises. Of particular concern will be the use of reductionist or instrumentalist methodologies to the generation of knowledge to inform educational practice such as through the inappropriate use of the randomised control trial (RCT).

I will then seek to move beyond critique and go in search of alternative infrastructures – different games – for approaching the problems that Hayek identified. Those problems are broadly seen as legitimate in our policy and practice contexts, so they cannot be ignored. My argument is that in the context we find ourselves in, we need infrastructures for educational policy making and leadership that provide adequate responses to Hayek's knowledge problem. However, those infrastructures need to do far less harm than the NPM. Finally, I will argue the merits of methodologies from the world of programme evaluation that leave a legitimate space for expertise when approaching problems of knowledge and working with those whose thinking is entrenched in the neoliberal *illusio*. An example of such a methodology is Contribution Analysis (CA; Mayne, 2011; 2012).

My argument is inspired by scholarship in the philosophy of science such as that of Callon et al (2009) in their explorations of 'technical democracy'. Exploring the intersections of 'capital S' Science and wider society, their work discusses the current inadequacies of what might be called the social infrastructures for decision making on socio-technical issues. In doing so, they promote a practical way forward – an infrastructure – of 'hybrid forums', in which experts and ordinary citizens come together to guide not only democratic decision making, but also scientific inquiry. Following such examples, I will argue for alternative infrastructures within education that do not *simply* treat educational knowledge as a proxy for price.

Notably, the search for alternative and viable solutions to Hayek's knowledge problem may actually be reasonably easy. It may require little more than acknowledging the hubris of the Anglosphere. An unfortunate part of working in a part of the world that uses the dominant language of scholarship on an everyday basis is that we start to think that the problems and solutions of English-speaking people are universal. As Biesta (2015) eloquently outlines in comparing the English and German language traditions, they are not. In the search for a different solution, I will start by simply looking at the different 'games' being played beyond the Anglosphere. While dominant in a group of countries including the United States, the United Kingdom, Australia and New Zealand, NPM is not the only solution to have been developed in response to the perceived need for a more outward-looking and responsive public sector. Other approaches to reducing bureaucratic rules and providing governance that is more reactive to the evolving needs of citizens have been used in other countries including *New Public Governance* (NPG; Dunleavy et al, 2006; Morgan and Cook, 2015) and the *Neo-Weberian State* (NWS; Pollitt and Bouckaert, 2011; Kopycinski and Mazur, 2017).

Theoretical fluency

Before we begin, some thoughts on theoretical framing. Following Rowlands and Rawolle (2013), the discussion so far has been rooted in the theoretical ensemble of Bourdieu. This is a powerful framework, but I am seeking to promote a wider discussion with colleagues including those whose scholarship is based within other frameworks. As such, I want to be a little more theoretically 'fluent', even if I lose a degree of nuance in the process. To this end, I will talk primarily of the 'infrastructures' of educational policy and practice. In doing so, I am not proposing new theory. By 'infrastructure' I mean something similar to the cluster of concepts that Bourdieu refers to as practice, actions and capitals (Bourdieu, 1996). However, I am referring also to related, if not entirely interchangeable, concepts in other theoretical frameworks such as Kemmis' (2019) idea of 'practice architectures', which develops from material dialectics; and the idea of socio-material assemblages we see in various applications of complexity theory (see, for example, Snowden, 2012), which typically arrives via Actor Network Theory (Latour, 2005). I am talking too of the focus on 'activity' arrived at through cultural historical theory (Engeström, 2006; Roth and Lee, 2007). Each of these theoretical positions, and others like them, offer unique and powerful insights. For my purposes here, however, I am interested in their similarities rather than their differences. Each of these frameworks talks to human action and human decision making occurring within a social and material context, and hence to being reliant upon an 'infrastructure'.

New Public Management is inadequate for acting in a complex world

For the present purpose at least, my core argument against NPM is simply that it provides an inadequate governance infrastructure for acting in complex educational environments. That is, even if one accepts the broad logics and philosophy of neoliberalism, their manifestation in NPM is sub-optimal. NPM simply does not meet the needs of educational practice. It is not fit for purpose, and it should be rejected out of hand.

In the NPM, public organisations – and this includes virtually all parts of mass education including most 'private' schools which are typically not viable without enormous subsidy from the state – are equated with private organisations. In order to encourage an entrepreneurial spirit, they are restructured with disaggregation, competition and incentivisation becoming the dominant policy tools (Barzelay, 2001). In this hegemonic formulation, the public sphere is presented as apolitical, and the role of government becomes the 'objective' and 'efficient' provision of services that cannot otherwise be provided by private organisations.

Despite the global systemic challenges of 2008 and 2020, NPM has remained the dominant public policy mechanism in education in many parts of the world, and notably the Anglophone countries (Wilkins et al, 2019; Barbana et al,

2020; Helgetun and Menter, 2020). Promoted under discourses such as 'school choice', our schools and universities remain disaggregated in quasi-competition, and wider policy objectives from literacy and numeracy improvement to the expansion of participation in higher education are approached through incentives such as competitive grants and 'reward' payments. These arrangements have not changed in decades, and the critique of the entire enterprise is well developed (see, for example, Lingard, 2020).

What has changed in the present century, though, is the social and systemic infrastructures that have entrenched the NPM in the states in which it was most advanced, the Anglophone states. From the outset of the reform movement that became the NPM, information was always essential. The advent of the internet and the rise of information sharing from the mid-1990s (Tronco, 2010), however, has allowed the NPM reformers to position many previously 'public' services – such as education – as 'consumer' services (Veale and Brass, 2019). This is now the orthodox thinking, what Bourdieuian scholars would call the *doxa*.

The role of information-sharing architectures has drawn attention from those thinking about educational policy specifically. In examining the use of business intelligence systems used by an Australian state education department, Sellar and Gulson (2019), for example, have drawn our attention to the way in which artificial intelligence is able to shape human decision making. This reflects a growing body of scholarship that invites us to see the systems we build not simply as aids to thinking but as part of the cognitive process (Hutchins, 2010). They argue that the business intelligence system can be seen as a part of the cognitive infrastructure of contemporary educational administration, and that it has a firm grasp on policy making in Australian education. This view is supported by arguments that data-driven educational policy challenges conventional wisdom in creating an 'enduring reliance on the precarious construction of objectivity as a key legitimator of policy-relevant scientific knowledge and "evidence-based" education governance' (Williamson and Piattoeva, 2019, p 64). In short, we have put great weight in proxies to guide our educational reforms and day-to-day decision making. The risk here – the potential 'tragedy of the proxy' – lies in the creation of illusionary educational entities that data analysis claims to represent objectively (Perrotta and Williamson, 2018).

In coining the term 'New Public Management', Hall (1993) argued that NPM was not simply a set of small changes in the way we do decision making due to learning by specialists and the public service. Rather, he suggested, it was a consequence of wider social learning – a paradigm shift. A central component of this paradigmatic social understanding, what Foucault (2017) might call a 'regime of truth', is a positivist understanding of the evidence in social decision making. NPM leaves no room for the politics of contested meaning making – rather, it thrives on simple, uncontested information. In a compelling argument, Davies (2019) has recently shown how this kind of reductionism has led to nation states and, increasingly, other organisations using information as 'intelligence' – in the sense of 'military intelligence' – rather than as the basis for deliberative knowledge building. Key in Davies' argument is the role that evolving information and communication technologies have played in this social direction. Information, he argues, is now moved around so rapidly that what is key is not the shared meaning making that this may allow, but what advantage it might give. In short, being first has replaced being best.

The risks of oversimplification

At issue in the educational policy context is the assumption in the automated thinking of the NPM that causal relations are implied from correlations that are 'additive, unifinal, and symmetrical' rather than complex and 'marked by conjunction, equifinality, and asymmetry' (Cilesiz and Greckhamer, 2020, p 333). This, I suggest, is where the NPM does much damage in education. Education is complex and nuanced, and the simple indicators chosen to allow for administration through market mechanisms as required in the reforms of the NPM are simply not sufficient. In contrast, a recognition of education's inherent complexity demands a move away from NPM and its state–society dichotomy towards an administrative model able to account for multiple discursive arenas in what is essentially a complex environment (Beckman, 2001).

A move towards understanding education as a complex environment in turn demands ways of representing educational practice not simply as a linear business process but as a cultural act whereby education enables, and is a consequence of, the human advantage of accumulating information stores that contribute to cultural learning, keeping shared knowledge, skills and experiences across society at optimal levels (Tomasello, 2016; and see Woolcott et al, 2019). It requires ways of representing the requisite 'skills, capacities, processes and practices' (Veale and Brass, 2019) needed to accommodate the ongoing development of educational policy in a complex environment where cultural learning and cultural accumulation require oscillation between person-to-person and person-to-information interactions, rather than interpretations and algorithm construction that is isolated from such cultural processes.

The empirical versus the real

The inadequacy of the NPM I have identified here is its tendency to grab hold of objectively observable proxies for a price signal and assume (hope?) that that proxy is a reasonable indicator of the quality of educational practice. In this model, professional expertise is essentially seen as irrelevant, or even as problematic.

The matter of expertise here is an important one. From its inception, neoliberalism has been an explicit rejection of expert knowledge (Hayek, 2014). As the primary founder of neoliberalism, Hayek's major contribution can be thought of as moving the central issue of economics from the 'distribution problem' to the 'knowledge problem'. The complexity of the knowledge problem – knowing what people want, what resources are available, how we should use those resources, who should get what, how people will react – he argued, should not be underestimated. It is too complex for central planners, for experts. In the context of his time – Hayek was writing in the mid-20th century – the failures of central planning evident in the communist states such as the USSR and China certainly appeared to lend some empirical support to this position. In the West, in contrast, it would take the stagflation crisis of the 1970s to give these ideas momentum via Thatcher, Reagan, and even under a notionally 'left-wing' *Labor* government in Australia. Prices and efficient free markets, Hayek argued, were superior to a reliance on experts when dealing with problems of knowledge.

The impact of this *illusio*, this game of price signals, on educational scholarship, research and professional practice has been immense. Questions of the purpose of education have been marginalised in favour of a focus on the 'efficient' delivery of 'what works'. One response to this need for an *apparently* objective proxy for price has been the rise of the RCT within education. With the idea of price in mind it is not surprising, perhaps, that the RCT has come to be seen in many policy forums as the 'gold standard' for educational research. In advising the Australian government on the best evidence base for education policy, for example, the Australian Productivity Commission (2016) took the position that '[t]he gold standard … is meta-analysis of randomised controlled trials and individual trials. Such approaches are the norm in health research, but they are seldom used in Australian education research'.

The pre-eminence of the RCT, however, has long been challenged even in the context of health research. Feinstein and Horwitz (1997), for example, argued for a distinction between evidence-based practice and 'best available' evidence. They noted that the gold standard of the RCT showed efficacy for the 'randomised' average patient, but 'not for pertinent subgroups formed by such cogent clinical features as severity of symptoms, illness, co-morbidity, and other clinical nuances' (Feinstein and Horwitz, 1997, p 529). In doing so, they point to studies that show that even in special academic medical settings, evidence from sources other than RCTs is used in therapeutic decision making. This is particularly so for decisions that 'involve etiology, pathophysiology, diagnosis, prognosis, mode of communication, and methods of reassurance, rather than a choice of specific therapeutic interventions' (Feinstein and Horwitz, 1997, p 530).

The essential arguments made by Feinstein and Horwitz – people are not 'average' and will have a range of confounding diseases, lifestyle choices and histories, and that compliance with therapy is difficult to separate from variables such as social support and patients' expectations and desires – resonate strongly in education (Winne, 2022). Meta-analysis of RCTs showing the effect size of diverse variables on learning simply does not speak to the interaction of those variables, and statistical attempts to combine them through techniques such as structural equation modelling quickly move past the expertise and interest of most practitioners. The result is that instead of this proxy for price helping us to understand and act within complexity, as Hayek proposed, we see instead the deployment of what might be thought of as evidence-based aphorism.

The influence of Hattie's (2009) meta-analytic work in Australia is a good example of evidence-based aphorism. This work suggests that teacher background and teacher practice combine to explain perhaps 30 per cent of the variance in student learning progress, with outside-of-school factors explaining much of the rest. In an apparent ignorance of the way percentages work, this has become a political mantra that teachers 'have the biggest impact on student learning' (see, for example, Ministers' Media Centre, 2023). At the base of this mantra, of course, there is the truth that what teachers do is the variable that can be most readily influenced by schools and educational policy makers. I am not taking issue with the finer detail of such meta-analysis here. That it shows, for example, that certain modes of student feedback are more useful than others is useful knowledge. There is clearly a place for this kind of research in the science of learning. The aphorism that teachers are 'important', though, really does not provide genuinely useful guidance for policy and leadership. When used this way, even when 'true', the empirical finding can actually obscure the real mechanisms they represent.

That aphorism might obscure the 'real' is not trivial (Rogers, 2015). The use of lists ranking the effect size of individual variables, for instance, is somewhat undone by research such as that from Musso et al (2012) who used the statistical technique of neural network analysis to show that multiple models of how pertinent variables fit together are needed to predict success for previously high performing students in mathematics compared to previously moderate performing students. That is, just as in the health context described earlier, the individuals we work with in education are not randomised averages.

RCT derived aphorism can also obscure the nuance of the test. In their meta-analysis of problem-based learning (PBL), for example, Dochy et al (2003) found that the effect size of PBL is strongly affected by the nature of the test. Specifically, they found that the effect size of PBL was much larger when the learning was assessed using methods requiring greater retrieval effort such as short answer or free recall questions, when compared to assessment based on recognition tasks such as multiple-choice tests. It is not surprising then that similar studies based only on machine-marked standardised testing suggest that PBL has only a small effect size. The nuanced advice not available through the linear orthodoxies of NPM here *might* be that if teachers are seeking to improve standardised test scores in the short term, then PBL is not advisable. If they are seeking to improve long-term retrieval, however, PBL should be considered.

The issues of representation are not restricted to how knowledge about learning is presented to educational professionals but are also evident in how it is presented by them. In recent decades, the educational narrative in many parts of the world has become dominated by the 'performance' of 15-year-olds in the international Program for International Student Assessment. Within this narrative, there has been a real sense that ranking lists, global numbers or grades can represent everything that is important in education. Certainly, a lot of work is done through marking rubrics and reporting checklists to provide a more detailed account of individual strengths and weaknesses in a particular piece of work, or across a course. Missing entirely from the standard form-driven apparatus, however, are ways to provide 'thick descriptions' (Geertz, 1973) of what is occurring in complex educational environments (Woolcott et al, 2021). Put simply, we lack the capacity to represent the richness of the sayings, doings and relatings (Kemmis, 2019) of our mass educational environments beyond the level of the tacit knowledge of teachers.

The lack of capacity I am pointing to here does not emerge from a complete lack of skill. Research discussing mosaic representations (for example, Chao and Moon, 2005; Coles, 2008; Hargreaves et al, 2009; Musso et al, 2012; Zolfaghari et al, 2016), shows a growing capacity for greater nuance. The social sciences and humanities have also given us many ways to generate detailed studies of many social environments – including education. Using such descriptions as part of larger scale decision-making, however, has proven difficult. Perversely, as technology has enabled us to collect more and more information about student learning, the situation has simply become worse. To cope with the large scale of data collection, the common approach has been to attenuate the descriptions of the world available by filtering out everything that is not considered important *a priori*. The difficulty is that in complex dynamic systems, knowing what is important can change rapidly. As Sellar and Gulson (2019) have argued, a pragmatic engagement with this technological infrastructure, and a subsequent revision of our choice of socio-technical infrastructure, must be a part of the way we do scholarship, policy making and leadership in education.

Breaking the *illusio* slowly

I will ground the argument of this next section by beginning with a story of the kind of experience that will be familiar to all who work in educational institutions.

> As a member of an 'expert' working group, I once provided the provost of one of the universities I have worked at with a literature review that raised significant concerns about the use of Student Evaluation of Teaching Surveys (SETS) that are widely used in higher education for the purposes of staff performance review, promotion and tenure. The issues raised included gender bias (Mengel et al, 2019), a tendency towards misinterpretation (Boysen et al, 2014), and findings that the instruments are wholly unreliable, showing little to no correlation with student learning outcomes (Uttl et al, 2017). The provost, an eminent scholar, researcher and educational leader, acknowledged each of these flaws without challenge to the underlying research. She then announced that the university would continue with its current SETS strategy, 'because we need to use something'.

I offer this anecdote first because it is another example of finding a proxy for price – do our students, as customers, find value in our teaching, even if that teaching is largely paid for by the state? More importantly for the purposes of this chapter, however, we offer it as a concrete example of how infrastructures shape our policy and practice in education. This educational leader was so firmly embedded in the *illusio* of the neoliberal university that she was entirely willing to make use of an instrument that she had just agreed was unreliable, invalid and deeply biased. An instrument that she would never accept in the context of peer review in research, or the examination of a thesis. Her specific choice of words was also important for the purposes of this essay: 'We need to use something.'

The idea that there is a need to use 'something' is critical to the strategy I am developing. In this anecdote, our expert group was able to outline all of the problems with the SETS system being reviewed, but we did not provide a viable alternative. In a similar fashion, the argument in this essay is that the collective work of our critical scholarship must provide alternative solutions to the problems *as identified by those who are currently deeply engaged with playing the neoliberal game*. We've been good at identifying the problems that neoliberalism and NPM create (Connell, 2013), and we've been good at arguing that the goals of the NPM are wrong (Anagnostopoulos et al, 2016). Too often, though, the changes we tend to call for require the outright disestablishment of the infrastructures of policy and leadership that our practitioners have been reliant on, probably for their entire careers. We are asking them to break the *illusio* instantly and to play another game with entirely new actions, capitals, architectures, assemblages and so on.

An alternative strategy is to make change slowly. To start moving towards a new game by starting with the 'prior knowledge' of those we seek to influence by first playing variations of the old. Within Bourdieu's game analogy, if the current game is a card game, then a move to massive online multiplayer computer game may be several steps too far. A move to a board game, however, may be familiar enough. The argument is for change, but change with small steps.

Small steps, non-linear games and the re-introduction of expertise

De-centring neoliberalism requires real and viable alternatives. As noted earlier, however, the search for such alternatives need not require invention. Alternative solutions to the fundamental problems Hayek identified can be found simply by looking beyond the Anglosphere. Despite its dominance in these countries and, hence, the pages of our prominent English language journals, neoliberalism and the NPM are not the only 'game in town'. They do not even frame the only game in the 'advanced' economies of the Organisation for Economic Co-operation and Development. Rather, in other places, and notably in Continental Europe, the 'Anglo-Saxon model' (Kopycinski and Mazur, 2017) has been considered, and has been found wanting. Where this has happened, alternative approaches to providing responsive governance have developed. Two examples are *NPG* (Morgan and Cook, 2015) and the *NWS* (Kopycinski and Mazur, 2017).

The scholarship around the NPG or the NWS often positions those models not simply as a parallel development, but rather as an explicit reaction to what is seen as the deficiencies of the 'Anglo-Saxon' model of NPM (Kopycinski and Mazur, 2017). That is, the countries pursuing these models have agreed with those promoting NPM that the classical Weberian state was in need of reform, but they have not agreed that the market-based models of business hold all of the answers and have sought to correct some of the problems that NPM has created.

NPG is a model that draws on network theory and is a natural landing point for those who understand educational practice in terms of complexity. NPG attempts to harness the capacities of modern information communication technologies to reach out beyond 'government' and include a wider range of social actors in policy development and implementation. It has been used quite widely by local government in the planning of inclusive urban services (Dahiya and Das, 2020). Like NPM, it rejects bureaucratic central planning. Rather than turning to price signals, however, it turns to building forums for collective deliberation. A particular point of divergence is the interest it brings to inter-organisational networking, alliance and collaboration that is not enacted through price and economic exchange (Osborne et al, 2013). Critics of NPG, however, have focused on problems related to accountability arising from the dispersal of powers a networked approach creates (Kopycinski and Mazur, 2017). The approach can also make decision-making processes protracted and costly.

NWS, on the other hand, draws together elements of NPM, NPG and even classic Weberian bureaucracy. Proponents of the NWS have reaffirmed the role of representative democracy, administrative law and the idea of public service. In short, the NWS sees a distinctive and 'steering' role for the state. On the other hand, it continues the interest of the NPM reformers in such things as prioritising a 'service delivery' orientation, citizens' wants and maintaining the use of performance management within the public service (Pollitt and Bouckaert, 2011). Compared to NPM, though, NWS asserts a greater role for expert knowledge in doing so. This has manifested in different ways in different European nations, but typically has led to both an increased emphasis on the professionalisation of the civic/public service, and a focus on improving the mechanisms and structures for public participation in decision-making processes.

The argument I am making is not for the uncritical uptake of either NPG or NWS as an infrastructure for educational governance in the Anglosphere. However, they do serve as a good starting point. They demonstrate that it is entirely possible to address Hayek's knowledge problem using means other than NPM-type policy making and leadership – that it is possible to develop governance that is responsive but retains a place for expertise within decision-making processes. The NPG and NWS approaches provide a diversity of alternatives to price as a way engage with and be responsive to the changing needs of the public, including the kinds of hybrid forums advocated by Callon et al (2009) discussed earlier in this essay.

When applied at the level of the individual institution, the NWS and NPG approaches call for an increasing, or, perhaps, a different kind of professionalism on the part of teachers and educational leaders. A professionalism informed by NWS/

NPG requires an engagement with the school community not as a 'market', but rather as a range of 'collaborators'. Within this framework, the expertise of educational professionals is vital, but the outcome is not one of separate groups of professionals competing for market share. Rather, the outcome is professionals collaborating *with* their community to create the hybrid forums that bring together people with different kinds of expertise and different kinds of knowledge to make decisions collectively and deliberatively.

Revealing the 'real'

The governance infrastructure that is NPM pushes us to deal with Hayek's knowledge problem by reducing our complex educational systems to simple empirical indicators. In both the NPG and NWS approaches we see alternative approaches to responding to that problem of knowledge, but that rely more so on collaboration than on competition. In essence, these approaches invite us to move away from the reductionism of NPM and to instead address the knowledge problem by seeking to understand more of the complexity of the real structures and interactions that occur within our educational spaces.

How we who work in education scholarship, policy making and leadership accept such an invitation requires careful thought and study. As I've noted earlier, for example, within the logics of governance systems such as NPM we have developed a tendency to rely more on intelligence that is fast over intelligence that is 'best', or even 'true' (Davies, 2019). The result is that the intelligence we use in making decisions about educational policy and practice has come to be dominated by knowledge generation within a positivist ontology. In short, at least within the Anglosphere, our wider social discourse has come to reject subjective interpretation – the market needs to know 'what works' and is not satisfied with the ambiguous answers. We have been playing the NPM game so long that this need is not likely to dissipate easily. As such, we need to think carefully about how we design any alternative governance infrastructures. We cannot ignore the needs of those currently playing the education game. We need to offer pragmatic alternatives.

My earlier critique of the RCT provides a good example of where alternatives are needed. The RCT is useful in its place, but within a complex setting like education where numerous goals, contexts and activities are engaged simultaneously, reductionist methodologies are simply inadvisable (Patton, 2012). We need to have clear and workable advice on an alternative, as invocations of 'teacher professional judgement' will not suffice in a socio-political context that has been conditioned to the certainty they appear to offer.

A viable alternative to the RCT – an example of the *kind* of design that can be more fully explored in education – is CA (Mayne, 2011; 2012). CA was developed in the context of programme evaluation as means of establishing casual relationships in contexts in which many exogenic variables interact and in which a simple and singular counterfactual cannot be established. It provides a systematic way to credibly assess cause and effect relationships in complex settings where contextual factors and complex interplay of actions are present (Buckley, 2016). The approach involves the attempt to verify the *theory of change* or *logic model* behind a programme/intervention, while simultaneously taking into consideration other influencing factors (Mayne, 2008; 2011; 2012; Lemire et al, 2012; Patton, 2012). This requires the clear and systematic building of a causal model to investigate (Barbrook-Johnson and Penn, 2022).

Rather than the simple accept/reject logic of more reductionist methodologies, CA is usually reliant on a multi-layered and multi-factored theory of change that is tested through the logical application of multiple forms of data in assessing what factors can reasonably be attributed to the dynamics of the system under investigation (Patton, 2015). As such, it provides a role for expertise, subjectivity and a pathway towards the exploration of the ontologies as well as axiologies of educational practice (Biesta, 2010). Also in sharp contrast to reductive approaches, CA endeavours to gather the best evidence to assess the impact of varied factors at each stage of a programme/intervention (Brentnall et al, 2018), and to explore alternative factors which may have been having significant influence (Lemire et al, 2012). In doing so, it provides support for exploring educational systems as complex and changing rather than fixed and mechanistic.

Pragmatic adaptive policy making

Certainty is alluring

I have taught more than one university course confidently bearing the phrase 'what works' in its title. *Aboriginal Education: What Works*, for example, was quite popular with the initial teacher education students and the external accreditation authority that had insisted that the uncertainty of (post-)colonial politics was irrelevant to closing the educational achievement gap of Australia's First Nations children. What was demanded, by the university students and accreditation authorities alike, was clear instruction on certain action. In short, they want to know what works.

Of course, in Aboriginal education as with almost any educational question, 'what works' is only ever a meaningful question when modified by considerations like 'for whom?', 'for what purpose?' and 'with what existing cognitive, social and cultural resources?' What good is it, for example, to adopt a strategy that improves basic skills results in numeracy and literacy testing if those same strategies also drive a disengagement with learning or, indeed, the learning environment?

It is these more complex questions, questions that may never have a simple and certain answer and for which price signals will never work, that demand a pragmatic and adaptive basis for policy making and leadership. The terms 'pragmatic' and 'adaptive' have been used here in their everyday sense, but also because they invoke the work of philosophers such as Dewey (1929) and more recent theorists drawing on complexity theory (Uhl-Bien et al, 2007) respectively. In their own ways, each of these traditions rejects certainty as a possibility in the context of complexity. However, they do not reject the use of information or the need to be responsive to changing needs expressed by the public. They point instead to a need for ongoing policy and leadership experimentation, and to collective meaning making in which the professionals take the voice of all stakeholders seriously (Snowden, 2012).

Pragmatic Adaptive Leadership and practice is qualitatively different to the way most educational institutions and systems in the English-speaking world now work (Fowler et al, 2022b). It asks our policy makers and leaders to step away from knowing what will work and, instead, to engage in an ongoing process of finding out what works in a certain time, in a certain place, with different and intersecting communities and agendas. Adopting such a mode of policy making and leadership, though, is no simple task. Complex systems are resilient. They tend to maintain their basic structure even when pushed far from their equilibrium, even when pushed by global crisis! In the English-speaking world, we have been playing the neoliberal *illusio* so long now that is it seared deep in our social thought and sustained in social and cognitive infrastructures. It is seared so deeply that many, if not most actors in our field will feel compelled to use 'something' to 'objectively' assure the quality and efficiency of educational 'services', even in the face of knowing that doing so can be quite destructive.

The difficulty of deliberately shifting a complex system is no better illustrated than by the ascendancy of neoliberalism itself. This was no fluke. Hayek, and others such as Friedman and Popper certainly wrote a compelling case in the academic and popular press, but there was more to it than this. As a now proliferating body of research shows, the development and growth of neoliberal thought was deliberate, well-funded and well-organised (Burgin, 2015; Mirowski and Plehwe,

2015). Through their Mont Pelerin Society and the influential networks they drew around themselves, they sought to actively persuade government, institutions and the public. It is likely and logical, therefore, that undoing this work will take an equally deliberate effort and strategy to shift the system. The provision of alternative educational decision-making infrastructures seems an essential part of such a strategy.

# THREE

Future-oriented learning

The remaining chapters of this book emerge from an ongoing and already long-running programme of research we have been undertaking with a school we refer to in our publications as Corroboree Frog College (CFC), who we met in the last chapter. We use frog species as pseudonyms for all our partner schools, quite at random. 'Corroboree', though, is an Australian word that is 'borrowed' from the Australian Aboriginal language *Dharug*, from the area now known as Sydney. It is a generic word for a meeting of Australian Aboriginal people, particularly for a ceremony or a celebration. As we've had many meetings and celebrations with this school, the name somehow seems apt. We should also note that it was teachers from this school who first described what we were doing as 'Pragmatic Adaptive Leadership', so it is also apt that this school should play a prominent part in this book.

CFC approached us with a remarkably open-ended challenge. They had done pretty well, they told us, at maximising student marks in the various external testing and credentialling systems. What they wanted to know now was, 'what else could we do to best prepare their students for life after school?'

This very open challenge highlights one of the hardest problems in leadership – where do we start? The school community could not know what it did not know, and to be frank, neither did we! Ultimately, though, 'life after school' is one of the principal problems that schools need to address every day. Like many researchers before us, our response was to begin by trying to build a *situational map* of the problem. It was in doing this that our *Theory of Pragmatic Adaptive Leadership* first began to emerge. In our previous collaborative research projects in other places, we have tended to build our situational maps using the principles of *Activity Systems Analysis* based on third generation Activity Theory (Yamagata-Lynch, 2010) or by using Bourdieu's (1977) theory of practice – also known as 'field' theory – as a starting point. The 'life after school' problem, however, was just too complex for us to make effective use of these mainstays of our research practice. For us, 'life after school' was the kind of runaway object that Engeström had described as being connected to many activities, or what might be seen as of interest to many of the semi-autonomous fields at the heart of Bourdieu's approach.

Indeed, this problem is so large that it requires more than one chapter, or an entire book perhaps, to cover it. Really, the problem could be framed as the 'what do we want from our schools?' problem. We will return to how we approached the methodological challenge of the 'life after school' problem in Chapter Five, but first let us look at how contemporary policy and research is attempting to address the 'life after school' problem. While the body of research and policy development outlined here provides an excellent foundation for future-oriented educational leadership, we will argue that it is useful but insufficient.

Education in an evolving world: the current state of the education system and the social needs it seeks to address

As a reader, you may have picked up this book because you were already wanting to make a change in schools, and we can tell you that you are not alone. Educational reform is a complex, evolving process that is frequently essential – but the critical question is, what should be the primary objective? We explore here the web of goals promoted by various academics and policy makers to try to make sense of the purpose of change. Essentially, this comes down to the types of knowledge, skills and capacities that we want our students to develop.

Mass education as it emerged from the industrial age has consistently held on to a linear concept of simply filling students' heads with useful knowledge. This industrial perspective treats education as a somewhat 'black box' process, such as in Figure 3.1. Students, other agents and resources are the inputs to the system and an educated citizen is the end outcome. In between is where the blend of art, science and magic known as teaching and learning come together in the complicated, yet determinate, process called education. This is a tantalising concept for politicians looking for easy to communicate answers and pitches for their next election cycle, but, as anyone who has been involved in the reality of education knows, it is a dramatic oversimplification.

Nevertheless, competencies that can be measured easily, and hence conveyed to the general public, have become important to all people working within education, mostly because they seem to provide clear metrics for improvement and highlight areas of need. An obvious example of this is the focus on NAPLAN in Australia, which attempts to measure aspects of literacy and numeracy.

Education, however, is much more than just the '3Rs' (Reading, wRiting and aRithmetic). It is a multidimensional construct that encapsulates a range of cognitive and

Figure 3.1: A black box view of the mass education process

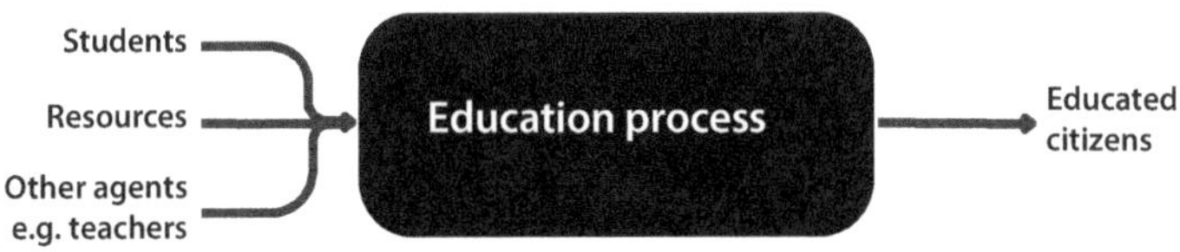

non-cognitive skills and knowledge that prepare students to be active citizens in society, and the understanding of this is what prompted CFC to ask their big question. In exploring these different dimensions, researchers and practitioners have developed many different frameworks to capture some of these nuances and to try to provide alternative or additional measures by which we can determine success.

21st-century skills

Coined around 2002 by the Partnership for 21st Century Learning (Trilling and Fadel, 2009), a term often used within education is '21st-century skills'. This is shorthand for those capacities that help students thrive in an ever-changing world and that augment the core subject knowledge learned in the classroom. These capabilities are often only vaguely defined and have been, arguably, ineffectively implemented in the first quarter of the century. As a replacement for the 3Rs, the key skills are commonly represented as the 4Cs; Communication, Collaboration, Creativity and Critical thinking (Partnership for 21st Century Learning, 2015). They are explored in many academic papers (González-Salamanca et al, 2020; Dishon and Gilead, 2021; Chen et al, 2022) and are promoted by educational bodies such as the United Nations Educational, Scientific and Cultural Organization (Scott, 2015), the World Economic Forum (2015) and the US National Research Council (2012).

These broad capacities are often discussed in the context of an increasingly technology-based economy and are positioned to meet the needs of the modern workforce, but they are also crucial to active participation in society outside of the workplace. Whether a student becomes an astronaut, a parent, a climate activist or all three, the 4Cs are applicable to almost all of their 'life after school'. So, recognising how impactful the 4Cs can be, how can they be incorporated into our situational map?

Communication

Learning is social, and students need to effectively express their ideas and potential misconceptions in this social environment. This requires opportunities to ask questions, interact with others, critically consider others' ideas and articulate their own reasoning. Of course, these skills don't always come naturally, so they may require explicit instruction and scaffolding from teachers.

Developing communication has often been seen as the job of English teachers, but the ability to express a range of ideas to a range of audiences for various purposes is relevant to, and crucial in, all subject areas. From the perspective of the situational map, this means that communication will appear and exert influence in multiple places within the education process – sometimes hindering and sometimes helping. While communication has long been a core skill taught in schools, the evolving landscape of digital communications – including the rise of social media and artificial intelligence – challenges us to adapt our teaching methods and prepare students to engage effectively with a diverse array of communication platforms and agents.

Collaboration

In a world that is becoming progressively more connected, the ability to empathise, coordinate and build on the strengths of others becomes highly important. We need these collaborative skills not just to tackle the big problems facing our planet, but also to learn and grow as individuals connected by our social bonds.

Collaboration is specifically important in an education context because our understanding of the world is largely shaped through interactions with others. After all, we can only see farther if we are able to stand on the shoulders of giants. If students struggle to engage meaningfully with their peers and teachers, they risk developing a blinkered view of the world, and may even miss out on valuable learning experiences. Consequently, this can hinder their ability to think innovatively, communicate across cultural boundaries and adapt to rapidly changing environments. This means we don't only collaborate for the sake of learning to collaborate, but we do it because it expands student learning in many subtle ways that are difficult to quantify. For our situational map this means we need to consider how the learning systems of individual students interact with each other and evolve to build those connections essential for success in life after school.

Creativity

Creativity has been valued as a skill for millennia, but understanding its cultivation has always been complex. To begin with, it is really quite difficult to define what creativity looks like. Is creativity the ability to come up with novel ideas, useful ideas or a mix of the two (Puryear and Lamb, 2020)? Is it a disposition, trait, product or, as the 21st-century skills suggest, a skill (Brainard, 2024)? Should it appear spontaneously or is it a consequence of hard work (Zedelius and Schooler, 2015)? Are we creative in only specific domains or is it a generic skill (Plucker and Beghetto, 2004)? What is generally accepted, however, is that creative solutions tend to emerge from processes rather than be deliberately designed by them.

These questions become crucial when we decide to foster creativity in our students. Among the 4Cs, creativity may be the most complex, as it significantly deviates from our industrial education model and does not fit neatly into either a traditional skills or knowledge box. Regardless, this difficulty does not diminish its importance. Students must transcend the past and envision future possibilities in order to navigate a complex and changing world. Our situational map needs to be flexible and robust enough to allow for unexpected behaviours to emerge without causing it to collapse.

Critical thinking

In a world where the very nature of truth is challenged (Chinn et al, 2020) and information is easily manipulated – and ever more so since the emergence of generative artificial intelligence – schools are often tasked with supporting critical thinking development (ACARA, nd). This is explored through multiliteracies such as critical literacy, critical numeracy and digital literacy, but there is often limited guidance on how teachers can actually operationalise this at developmentally appropriate points (Huang and Sang, 2023). To address this gap, educators are turning to pedagogies that emphasise problem-solving and critical analysis.

Pedagogies such as problem-based learning, project-based learning or design-based learning encourage both imagination and the careful consideration of information in order to meet (often) predetermined goals. This makes these practices valuable for developing both critical and creative thinking. The teaching and practice of problem solving is often aimed at building deeper engagement with knowledge through active, constructive and interactive learning (Chi and Wylie, 2014), where the hope is to mirror authentic situations and also to leverage generative learning processes (Fiorella, 2023). However, challenges lie in creating learning environments that provide scaffolded support for a diverse student community, while still effectively integrating critical thinking and problem-solving skills. This nuanced task requires educators to balance structured guidance with opportunities for independent exploration and requires our situational map to be able to capture and account for personalised learning.

Organization for Economic Co-operation and Development transformative competencies

The 4Cs don't exist in isolation. As we have shown, they're all connected to each other and to different forms of knowledge, as well as being shaped by students' attitudes and values. This complex web of abilities helps learners navigate both the school world and the even more complex world of life after school.

However, when examined closely, we see that these skills are still heavily influenced by the perceived needs of employers rather than the more general needs of society. The Organization for Economic Co-operation and Development (OECD) has taken a different tack and investigated how these skills can interact to form three so-called 'transformative competencies' which will help us build a better world (OECD, 2020). These transformative competencies can be thought of as broad aims for education that help students meet the challenges of the future. They are identified as being: creating new value, reconciling tensions and dilemmas, and taking responsibility (Figure 3.2).

Creating new value is described as blending 'a sense of purpose with critical thinking and creativity' (OECD, 2019). It engages with entrepreneurship while recognising the importance of environmental, economic and social responsibility. The concept of managed risk and resilience towards achieving personally set goals is central to this particular competency.

Reconciling tensions and dilemmas explores the nuance of balancing competing demands to achieve goals that benefit the world. This balancing act clearly utilises communication and collaboration skills but equally requires critical thinking and creativity to navigate often contradictory ideas and find positions of compromise.

Taking responsibility leans into how we make choices ethically. Diverting away from the workplace focus at the heart of 21st-century skills, this competency leans heavily on the place critical thinking has in ethical reasoning. Not all goals are worthy of the sacrifices needed to achieve them, but taking responsibility means being aware of this trade off in *all* the decisions we make.

By highlighting these competencies, the OECD is explicitly acknowledging that attitudes and values such compassion and

Figure 3.2: A representation of the Organization for Economic Co-operation and Development's transformative competencies framework

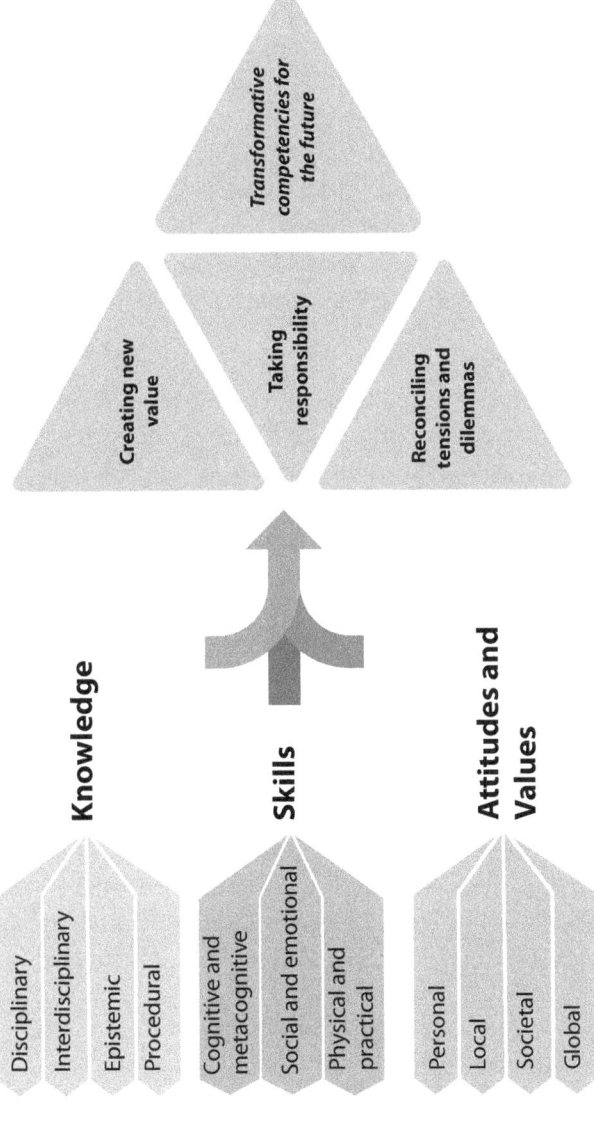

respect are just as important as cognitive skills and content knowledge. This poses additional challenges for our situational map given that the former of these frequently receives far less attention in modern curriculum and success metrics.

These two key skills frameworks serve to highlight many of the internal tensions and contradictions that exist within the black box of Figure 3.1. They also act as a warning that, when working with complex systems such as education, one plus one may not always equal two.

Operationalising learning in a complex world

So how does a school leader deal with, and more so operationalise, the competing priorities of the complex process that we have just outlined and that we call learning?

As many teachers instinctively know, the 4Cs are alive and well in the classroom, and they are implemented by essentially drawing on aspects that are present in curriculum documents. However, they are also underrepresented in metrics that determine school achievement, and so can feel invisible, less important, or even like optional extras.

The transformative capacities add yet another layer of complexity when we start to consider what types of *people* we need to develop to support a healthy society. How can we look at the little boy entering the classroom on his first day on school, wide-eyed and excited, and envision ways to foster the ethical reasoning he will use to make his own medical decisions? How do we map the pathway for the 13-year-old girl, who will one day have to make empathetic choices around neighbourhood issues? What about for every student – and we mean *every* student – who will one day inherit, and care for, an increasingly complex and forever dynamic world?

Many researchers over the years have attempted to answer the question we posed at the beginning of this section and many solutions have been proposed. We, however, will briefly focus on the synthesis of learning science research carried out by Darling-Hammond et al in their quest to understand how to 'promote children's well-being, healthy development, and transferable learning' (Darling-Hammond et al, 2020, p 98). This team's Science of Learning and Development (SoLD) framework highlights many of the elements the research community has proposed to support the development of the complex types of competencies and skills discussed previously.

They begin by considering education systems as consisting of four interrelated aspects of quality education which each encompass a set of principles of practice. These principles in turn all surround the whole child, emphasising the holistic nature of learning. These four SoLD aspects are outlined as follows.

Supportive environments

A supportive environment is one of safety, belonging and trust, and is closely linked to students' need for connection with teachers and peers. It targets both the school community and individual classrooms as crucial channels for fostering support. Trust among staff, students and parents is built by acknowledging and celebrating a culturally responsive learning community. The approach promotes consistent classroom practices and structured routines that reduce student anxiety and enhance learning.

Productive instructional strategies

Within these supportive environments, students engage in rich, authentic tasks that integrate explicit instruction and guided inquiry. Prior knowledge serves as a springboard for active learning, encouraging students to question, propose and justify ideas. This student-centred approach, emphasising conceptual understanding and motivation, is coupled with developing learning-to-learn skills. Formative feedback allows students to assess their progress towards learning goals and identify areas for improvement. Additionally, emphasis is placed on metacognitive instruction and reflection to build transferable strategic knowledge.

Social and emotional development

Tied closely to wellbeing, this aspect aims to prepare students to have the academic buoyancy to overcome obstacles and persist in their learning. It focuses on the explicit development of socio-emotional skills while promoting productive mindsets which support resilience and a positive view of learning.

A system of supports

The importance of integrated services which support the types of learning they have described in the other areas must not be overlooked. These multi-tiered support systems help to address obstacles to learning both within the classroom and in the wider community.

We have established that the number of considerations impacting leaders' choices regarding building a robust and effective school are numerous. How do we balance what employers want, what society needs and what learning science tells us is critical? This may seem like an impossible task; however, if we step back and look at the true nature of what is being asked of the education system, then we can start to see that not everything described needs to be explicitly acted on. Using the framing of activity theory briefly explored in Chapter One and represented simply in Figure 3.3, we see that some of the described elements are tools, some are objects of transformation and some are outcomes. In some cases, elements fit into multiple categories as shown in Table 3.1.

We commend Darling-Hammond et al (2020) for their synthesis of a model aiming to encompass all educational goals; however, we feel that, as with other similar efforts, subtle yet significant insights can be overlooked when consolidating a

Figure 3.3: The elements of an activity system

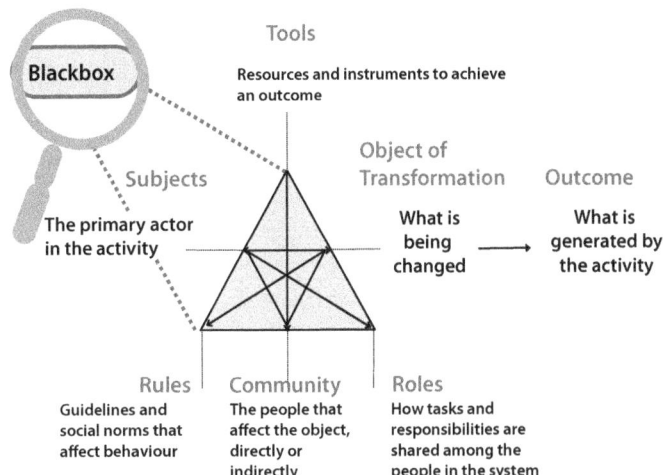

complex field of knowledge. From the Pragmatic Adaptive Leadership perspective, this includes mislabelling tools and objects of transformation as outcomes in the SoLD model. By framing all elements of learning as outcomes, actionable steps can be obscured, and the systems of change reduced to magical black boxes. To construct a model for genuine change, the focus needs to be on the objects that require transformation to enable the emergence of the outcome. This approach shifts us away from vague concepts, like 21st-century skills – which are easy to reference but challenging to implement – and towards the development of activity systems that drive desired transformation in the object.

Enacting change

No professional development programme, system mandate or curriculum alone can fully equip teachers for the level of complexity we have outlined in this chapter. Instead, we

Table 3.1: Mapping of framework elements to activity system objects

Framework		Element	Tool	Object	Outcomes
21st-century skills		Communication	✓	✓	
		Collaboration	✓	✓	
		Creativity	✓	✓	
		Critical thinking	✓	✓	
Transformative competencies		Creating new value			✓
		Reconciling tensions and dilemmas			✓
		Taking responsibility			✓
SoLD	Supportive environment	Trust and connections among staff and families			✓
		Classroom learning communities	✓		
		Structures for effective caring	✓		✓
	Productive instructional strategies	Student-centred instruction	✓		
		Conceptual understanding and motivation		✓	✓
		Learning how to learn	✓		✓
	Social and emotional development	Integration of social-emotional skills	✓		
		Development of mindsets	✓		
		Educative and restorative behavioural supports	✓		
	System of supports	Extended learning opportunities	✓		
		Co-ordinated access to integrated services	✓		
		Multi-tiered systems of support	✓		

need to purposefully cultivate educational leaders who not only understand these factors but who are committed to engaging in learning design and experimentation to discover which practices work for their context, students and particular topic or task they are exploring. They need to be aware of the importance of some of the outcomes highlighted in this chapter, but also be clear that outcomes can emerge from the activity of the classroom and that therefore their focus should be on the objects of transformation.

This type of transformation is often framed as being driven by empirically supported pedagogies, suggesting a consensus among researchers and educators. However, such agreement is rarely universal. While leaders often have a shared recognition of the value of outcomes like those outlined in the SoLD, 21st-century skills, or the OECD transformative competencies, different approaches are considered effective in achieving these outcomes. What is frequently overlooked in this simplification is that outcomes often emerge from a variety of activities. Practices that may seem incongruous – such as explicit direct instruction and inquiry-based approaches – can contribute to outcomes like 'conceptual understanding and motivation'. The critical task for the pragmatic adaptive leader is to be clear on the outcome and select the practices most appropriate to lead to appropriate objects of transformation while carefully navigating potential tensions to ensure effective implementation.

Self-regulated learners

By way of illustration, we will explore the concept of self-regulated learning (SRL) as it could be applied to a school like CFC. This is an important application for us as one of our earlier projects with CFC led to the creation of the learning model that they have implemented across the school.

SRL is often reduced to the phrase 'learning to learn' in the same way that a related concept, metacognition, is frequently summarised as 'thinking about thinking'. Neither of these truly describes the complexity of either construct but they provide a vague concept of the outcomes that SRL delivers – students who have the capacity to flourish not only within school but across their whole life through careful consideration of their own learning processes.

SRL has a long history within the learning sciences (Schunk and Greene, 2017), resulting in copious models exploring the many nuances and complexities of a fairly intricate construct. The complexity of this construct, however, is one of its greatest strengths. The development of SRL relies on multiple interconnected factors or objects of transformation, including the learner's motivation, emotions, metacognitive skills and cognitive abilities, along with environmental supports that foster agency and reflective practices. SRL, therefore, requires an educational mindset that promotes lifelong learning, reflexive thinking and strategic goal setting and attainment, rather than relying on a set of context-dependent 'shortcuts' prone to misapplication. Essentially, the learning sciences view of how a human develops.

The richness of this theory has contributed much to the learning sciences, but this richness also comes with a cost. SRL is not necessarily well understood by the lay-person and is thus difficult to purposefully develop. We will discuss three foundational models for SRL in the following sections, and in doing so, build up a common understanding of the objects, tools, rules and other resources needed to implement SRL in a school like CFC.

To begin this task, we suggest you follow along with the diagram in Figure 3.4 that describes the complex system that is SRL. It is presented as a broad overview of three major theories but emphasises that content and even skills are only the tip of the iceberg when considering learning. In the following sections we will break this down a little to show some of the key interactions.

Zimmerman's models of self-regulated learning

Zimmerman's theories of self-regulation have been foundational for many subsequent SRL models. Building on the socio-cognitive theories of his colleagues, Albert Bandura and Ted Rosenthal, Zimmerman explored various theoretical aspects of SRL, which were refined over years of research (Panadero and Alonso-Tapia, 2014; Panadero, 2017). His first model (Zimmerman, 1989) explored the interrelation between the person, the environment and their behaviour. As shown in Figure 3.4, the connection to the environment highlights how our context can influence our actions, while we can also see a clear link between our identity and how we regulate our behaviour. Essentially Zimmerman highlighted the complex situation we have expanded on within this book.

Zimmerman's second model (Zimmerman, 2000) is represented at the centre of interaction between the student and the task, mediated by metacognitive regulation. Metacognition is at the centre of this diagram as it is a key process, with some researchers describing it as 'the engine of self-regulated learning' (Winne, 2022, p 773). Essentially, metacognition describes the consideration of your own thinking and the purposeful control of it to achieve our goals (Flavell, 1979).

In Zimmerman's conception, students go through processes of forethought, performance and reflection – they complete a self-regulation loop – each time they interact with a task. This categorisation has helped to identify the different types of thinking required by students and shifted the focus from the products of learning to its processes. Functionally, Zimmerman challenges teachers and learners to engage more fully with how they learn, rather than solely focusing on what they learn.

Boekaerts' broader conceptualisation of self-regulated learning

Boekaerts, working during the same period as Zimmerman, extended the understanding of SRL by shifting the focus to incorporate the impacts of emotion on learning. She explored not just what students did, but what motivated them to employ specific strategies.

Figure 3.4: A representation of the self-regulated learning system

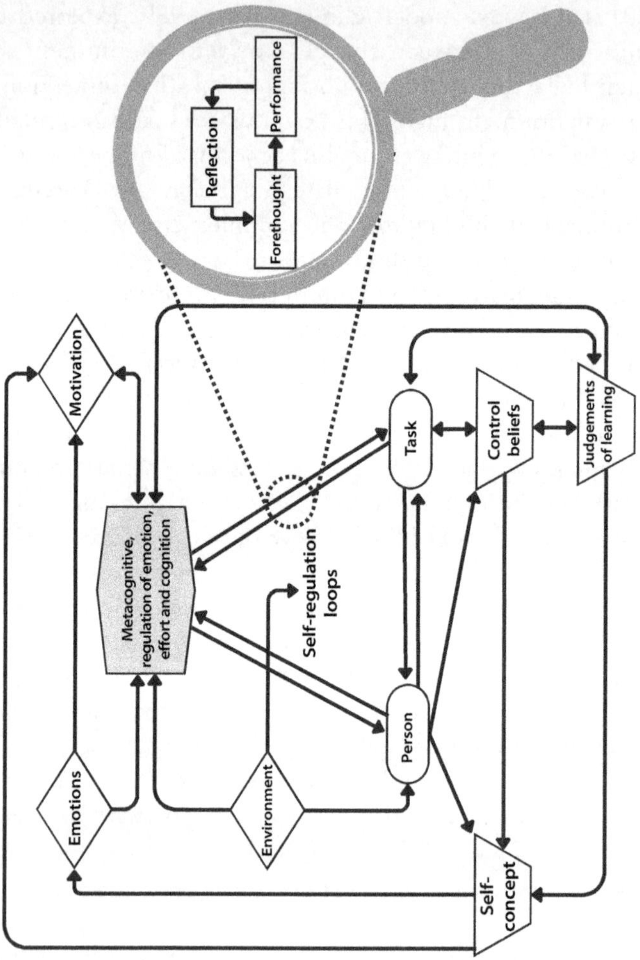

Boekaerts' dual processing self-regulation model (Boekaerts, 2011) is represented in Figure 3.4 by the interaction of motivation, emotions and metacognitive regulation in the upper half of the diagram. This connection moved SRL beyond mere knowledge and skill acquisition and emphasised wellbeing as a crucial component of a student's learning journey. It also reveals feedback loops driven by the student's experiences. For example, when a learning situation feels threatening, students may experience negative emotions that prioritise protecting their wellbeing, often at the expense of motivation to learn. Conversely, students who perceive learning as achievable and supported are more likely to pursue mastery goals, engaging in metacognitive strategies that enhance both their learning and their motivation to learn.

Boekaerts' model moved beyond the dominant learning theories of the time, which were drawn from clinical psychological experimentation focused heavily on cognitive elements (Schunk, 2020). While these theories, such as Cognitive Load Theory (Sweller, 1994), have seen substantial backing through numerous randomised controlled trials and other experimental methods, they often fail to recognise that the key role that motivation and emotions play is not solely the direction of effort, but the enhancement of capacity to engage in cognitive and metacognitive processes, too (Zheng et al, 2023). Essentially, Boakaerts helps to highlight other objects of transformation that also need to be considered when trying to promote positive academic outcomes.

Efklides' 'Metacognition and Affect in Self-Regulated Learning' model

Efklides' 'Metacognition and Affect in Self-Regulated Learning' (MASRL) model (Efklides, 2011) expanded this further. In Figure 3.4, this is illustrated by the explicit inclusion of self-concept and control beliefs and by the acknowledgement that metacognitive regulation extends beyond cognition and emotions to encompass the regulation of effort as well. Like

Boekaerts, Efklides saw that historical experiences and their related emotions were a key driving force in how we acted in the future. That is to say, how we perceive our abilities and how we have tackled similar tasks before directs how motivated we are to engage and how we regulate ourselves.

The MASRL model identifies and explores the interaction between two levels of functioning: the task level and the person level. The student's self-concept, affect, ability, control beliefs, motivation and metacognitive knowledge and skills are carefully considered in the light of what the task is asking and which learning process is required to tackle the task. During the learning, students activate cognitive patterns, engage in metacognition and attempt to regulate affect and effort.

Efklides' model provides important insights into the criticality of considering both the personal characteristics of the learner and the design of the learning environment and learning tasks. It distinguishes between states – temporary conditions – and traits, which are more permanent characteristics. Educators can focus on the state emotions, metacognitive knowledge and motivations of students, but it is important to understand that not all learning tasks elicit the same responses. There is a difference between a student who suffers an all-encompassing mathematics anxiety and one who is triggered by particular concepts in mathematics that interact negatively with their self-concept, ability or prior experiences. Efklides' work challenges us to design learning tasks that not only teach self-regulatory processes but also consider the individual student and encourage reflection on experience to shape their engagement with learning. Her contributions expand our understanding of the activity systems involved in learning and the diverse objects of transformation within these systems.

Nurturing a self-regulated learner

These three theories highlight important objects for transformation that schools can target. As a pragmatic adaptive leader, the way we view a learner's processes needs to expand beyond purely cognitive activities to include the dispositional and affective elements of their learning. Values such as flexibility, mindfulness and iterative learning begin to intertwine with traditional values like focus and persistence. A self-regulated learner therefore becomes the model of what a future citizen who can thrive in life after school should be.

How, then, do we promote the necessary activity systems to cater to our current students in preparation for their futures? We need learning environments that transcend industrial-age education, where learning outcomes were measured by often arbitrary metrics of skills for current employment. The new approach requires educators to differentiate assessments based on individual student learning goals, with teachers serving as scaffolders for the development of these goals and as identifiers of effective learning strategies that students can experiment with and hone themselves against through carefully constructed learning activities.

Motivation to engage with learning

One of the key objects of transformation within each of the SRL models we have explored is motivation. Understanding strategic learning cycles holds little value without the willingness to invest effort and persist through challenges. There are many influential theories of motivation that intertwine with the development of SRL but within this book we will focus specifically on Self-Determination Theory (SDT, Deci and Ryan, 1985; Ryan and Deci, 2020) as our theoretical framework due to the clarity of purpose it gives when progressing through the Pragmatic Adaptive Leadership process.

SDT distinguishes between two types of motivation: intrinsic motivation, which drives pursuit of mastery goals and aligns naturally with SRL processes, and extrinsic motivation, which stems from external rewards like grades or the desire to avoid punishments such as social consequences or school-imposed sanctions like extra schoolwork. While extrinsic motivation can provide an incentive, Ryan and Deci (2020) argue that its impact varies greatly, ranging from supporting intrinsic motivation to driving complete disinterest. For example, grades are often seen as rewards for hard work and ability, and they can be in the short term for some students – but if a student does not achieve the desired grade, then they may feel shame or lack of interest leading to disengagement.

Intrinsic motivation, on the other hand, has repeatedly been identified as underpinning achievement at school and overall wellbeing (Taylor et al, 2014; Bradshaw et al, 2022; Yu et al, 2023). This is not surprising when we consider the factors impacting the SRL models. Students find it hard to set learning goals, develop strategies and reflect on their learning journey if they are not focused on mastering their learning. SDT offers a particularly relevant framework for education by identifying three key conditions necessary to foster intrinsic motivation: autonomy, competence and relatedness.

Autonomy refers to students' agency in directing their own learning. This requires teachers to implement practices such as connecting classwork to students' personal experiences and interests, allowing students to help define success criteria and positioning themselves as learning partners rather than mere instructors (Reeve and Cheon, 2024). While many educators recognise the value of this student-centred approach, they often face constraints from established practice architectures embedded at classroom, school and system-wide levels.

Competence perceptions are intertwined with self-efficacy, confidence and realistic goal setting. Feelings of competence develop when learners can accurately assess task requirements and understand their own capabilities. Supportive classrooms foster competence by managing cognitive load effectively through supportive structures (Evans et al, 2024), providing appropriate challenges (Perry et al, 2007) and reframing mistakes as learning opportunities (Metcalfe, 2017; Steuer et al, 2024). However, balancing these educational practices can be challenging. For example, while scaffolding helps build competence, excessive control of a student's learning may undermine autonomy. Conversely, insufficient scaffolding can diminish said student's sense of competence.

The final element of intrinsic motivation is relatedness expressed by teachers who show care, empathy and respect (King et al, 2024). Schools are social spaces in which we build our understandings through our interactions with others (Bandura, 1986). We share ideas, reconfigure our thoughts, celebrate successes and seek support within them. It is no wonder, therefore, that students who have this connection often have higher levels of wellbeing and achievement (León and Núñez, 2013; Stiglbauer et al, 2013). The problem often arises when students lack this relatedness, or the strategies in which to achieve connection, leading to lack of engagement with school and further disconnection.

All three of these aspects of motivation are clearly key, but are also difficult to balance and address within current school models. SRL is highly supportive of each element and develops as a result of meeting the motivational needs of students. We now, therefore, consider how we can start this virtuous cycle using Pragmatic Adaptive Leadership.

Conclusion

In this chapter, we have explored CFC's open-ended challenge of preparing students for life after school – a challenge that is clearly multifaceted and nuanced. Traditionally, education has been seen as a linear input-output style of process, where the 'magic' that happens inside the black box is nebulous and obscured. While there are many theories about the complex capabilities that a thriving adult uses to participate in society, these are often described as tools or outcomes. Instead, we have argued that they need to be thought of as specific, transformable objects that can be grappled with as part of an activity. And so, our journey with CFC began by peeking inside the black box of the everyday practices and activities that happened inside the college to really ask 'what is the current situation?'

This Situational Mapping led us to co-developing an education model with CFC that targets these more complex and more difficult-to-define objects of transformation so that together we could begin to move away from the intangible to the tangible and start paving the way to make goals and activities truly actionable. In the next chapter, we will examine the obstacles to change and begin to outline strategies for building activity systems that support the objects of transformation and the desired outcomes we have discussed.

FOUR

The complexity of learning contexts

In Chapter Two, we set out a case asking school leaders to step away from certainty in favour of an ongoing process of finding out what works at specific times and places, especially when there are intersecting communities and agendas. Then, in Chapter Three, we highlighted important outcomes for schools requiring this leadership. In this chapter we will build some of the 'infrastructure' to respond to this challenge.

At its heart, Pragmatic Adaptive Leadership (PAL) is an approach to modelling complex systems as we lead change. Pragmatic Adaptive Modelling (PAM)'s approach to modelling is built upon the theoretical ensemble outlined in this chapter. Here, we explore different ways of thinking in 'systems', rather than a linear approach to school leadership, and where that sits in the wider scholarship of education. It will outline how theories of practice, activity and complexity each provide ways to explore education as a system with many moving parts, and have each contributed to PAL, before introducing much of the PAL approach.

As our discussion moves into the theory and method of modelling, we'll largely leave the critical scholarship of Chapter Two behind. The link is important, though, and we ask that you keep it in mind. Educational work is currently undertaken largely in institutions that are subject to neoliberal governance. That is, our institutions are essentially understood as service providers competing in a market, and so they need a measure to compete for. It has long been recognised that making any measure or indicator into a goal will tend to distort and corrupt the process it is intended to monitor (Campbell, 1979). Nevertheless, our governance systems call for measures, and while we generally agree with the critique of the entire neoliberal approach, we do not see this demand being replaced any time soon. What we do hope is that we as researchers, allied with thoughtful and knowledgeable school leaders, might be able to shift the focus from simple and blunt measures towards measures that actually monitor the real complexity of the systems we work with. It is with this in mind that we turn to some of the theories that help us model social systems like education.

Theories of practice

Practice theories, in their various forms, are a common way that scholars have sought to understand education as something that occurs within a social system. Practice theory emerged in the social sciences in the 1970s, when scholars (Bourdieu, 1977; Giddens, 1979; Schatzki, 1996; Peck et al, 2021) sought to better explain the development and change of 'practices' – or ways of doing things – like law (hence 'legal practice'), medicine or teaching. Practice can even be involved in how we participate in less formal things, like religious worship of the playing of music.

More often than not, the way we actually do things in the world is completely different from how things work on paper, because our actions are influenced by much more than just cognitive process. There are many different 'streams' of practice theory, each with its own focus and differences in detail, but they share a central realisation – practices do not happen in isolation but are interconnected (Schatzki, 2019), and they are context-specific.

Bourdieu's field theory

One of the more celebrated theorists of practice is Pierre Bourdieu, a French sociologist and public intellectual who envisaged a broader sociological understanding of practices. Bourdieu's framework has been applied to schooling extensively (see, for example, Lowrie and Jorgensen, 2012; Lingard et al, 2015; and ourselves in Chapter Two of this book). It highlighted that focusing only on cognitive processes is insufficient for understanding why human systems act in the way they do (Fogle and Theiner, 2018). Instead, Bourdieu aimed to understand the social world by exploring often implicit elements of the ways human interact.

A central part of this practice theory was the idea of *field* – a structured social space with its own rules and norms, such as the academic, economic and cultural fields. In each field individuals have *capital* determining their relative status and position. In the field of education this would include cultural capital (knowledge that helps you work in a specific environment), social capital (the sum of your social networks and the related benefits) and symbolic capital (what you can do because of your own prestige or recognition). You could imagine this through a student in a small primary school who has strong relationships with their teachers and peers and a deep understanding of the implicit rules of the school. This child would thrive and be engaged in this context because of their high social capital, but when they shift to high school, where they don't have pre-established relationships and the rules are very different, they may struggle. This is often due to the lowered capital reserves resulting from the shift in field.

Another central tenet of Bourdieu's work is the concept of *habitus*, which is particularly relevant in education, and the types of work that we are highlighting with PAL. Habitus describes how we behave due to our worldviews and social conditioning from the field around us, which inevitably drives our future practices (Grenfell, 2014). These 'durable, transposable dispositions' (Bourdieu, 1977, p 72) determine our ways of acting, feeling, thinking and being, which will be replicated to different fields over time (Grenfell, 2014). These habits of the mind are often so deeply ingrained that they prevent change, such as when a student who deliberately engages in disruptive behaviour for attention acts as the 'class clown' right throughout their entire formal education, or when a highly experienced teacher defaults to traditionalist pedagogies because 'that's how it has always been done at this school'. This means habitus is often subtle and invisible at a surface level, but emergent behaviours can be identified through analysis. It is, of course, difficult to affect habitus, but the good news is that it is not fixed and so can be slowly adjusted through intentional changes to the field.

Bordieuan theory has played an important part in identifying the underlying dynamics within education – particularly the unequal access to social and cultural capital within fields that can impact behaviour and, therefore, students (Murphy and Costa, 2015). It has helped to conceptualise often implicit constraints and affordances, and we celebrate the excellent scholarship that has made use of this framework, but this can lead to impractically heavy analysis. It enables us to reveal the invisible structures of 'what is' but it doesn't help us to make impactful decisions, nor does it

resonate with the simplistic neoliberal metrics of success that still inevitably impact us.

Kemmis' practice architectures

Another notable scholar of practice is the Australian Stephen Kemmis. His work can be read as a continuation of Bourdieu's project, with a focus on the fields of practice that occur within education, where he has been interested in mapping out habitus to find ways to change it. Central to this approach is the principle that what we *do* means more than what we *say* (Mahon et al, 2017). Kemmis therefore divided practices into (cultural-discursive) sayings, (material-economic) doings and (socio-political) 'relatings' (Kemmis et al, 2014a). This provided an observable way of exploring what is happening in the classroom and implied that learning is presented as a process of initiation into practices (Kemmis et al, 2014b). That is to say, in Kemmis' conception the process of learning is not about the acquisition of a body of knowledge but rather it becomes a process of understanding and, indeed, embodying a series of practices and how to apply them. Bourdieu's conception of field, therefore, becomes a much simpler idea of practice as a 'place' where sayings, doing and relatings happen (Kemmis, 2019). Kemmis refers to this place as the practice 'architecture'.

In Kemmis' approach, practice architectures define and govern practices. It shapes practice, but is also shaped by practices (Mahon et al, 2017). Careful consideration of these practice architectures is used to identify what is constraining particular desired practices and methods, and to open up pathways to change (Kemmis, 2019).

Applying this to a whole school, it is evident that there are many places where roadblocks can occur. The physical realities of a school's material-economic situation, such as its facilities, technological resources, layout, geographical position or funding structures require practical decisions that can disrupt or enable change, and so cannot be ignored when leading a school. Similarly, the school is bound by socio-political arrangements, such as curriculum, policy, school board governance, parental pressure and power structures that impact not just what is taught, but how it is taught and who makes those decisions. Finally, there are cultural-discursive aspects which shape (and are shaped by) educational beliefs and philosophies, accepted pedagogies and traditional modes of acting. The latter practice architecture can be particularly difficult to shift, resulting in the stagnation of teaching practice.

Practice architectures in action

To illustrate this concept, we will draw on one of our early collaborations with Corroboree Frog College. In this early project our focus was on a new centre that had been built to support the teaching of Science, Technology, Engineering and Mathematics (STEM) subjects. This technologically enhanced teaching environment had access to many flexible and powerful tools for learning and was built to encourage new teacher practices that would engage students deeply in new ways of learning. To encourage student-centric pedagogies, many of the classrooms were designed to be adaptable, where furniture could be easily moved, walls could be opened for bigger spaces, and there were multiple electronic whiteboard screens that the students could view and utilise to show their work. Teachers were invited to come and take advantage of this innovative learning space through a booking system.

But despite all these affordances, we actually observed that many teachers reverted to the material economic practices that were common to their regular classrooms. Even though the spaces were not as constricting as a traditional school science lab, with its bolted down desks facing the teacher, the computers in the labs still had to be powered, which meant they faced the wall and restricted collaborative work. A follow-on effect was that teachers tended to walk around behind the students and provide input into their processes, thereby continuing the entrenched teacher-led learning and socio-political practice architectures of their regular classrooms.

In other rooms, laptops allowed the space to be more adaptable, so the students were able to be grouped in a more collaboration-friendly way. Nevertheless, the cultural-discursive and socio-political practice architectures still created roadblocks to change. Even though the lessons were no longer ostensibly teacher-led, students still showed very low agency and so relied heavily on the computer program, meaning the lesson ultimately became 'device-led'. Instead of building the socio-constructivist environment of deeper engagement originally envisaged, the students' interactions (with teacher and device) were still based around cycles of instructions, which prevented the deep thinking ordinarily developed through meaningful discussions and problem solving. Unintentionally, the material economic practice architectures of collaborative desk arrangements simply provided students the opportunity for off-task behaviour, rather than true and meaningful interaction.

It was evident then that the teachers' pedagogical reasoning was still being constrained by the habitus of the regular classroom. They hadn't yet adopted new patterns of teaching and learning that would suit this new environment and its many affordances because they focused more on the technicalities of the tools than on how learning could be facilitated by the tool or how to scaffold practices that supported this (Fowler and Leonard, 2021). Here, it is evident that improving teaching doesn't simply flow from changing the environment but rather from nurturing the pedagogical reasoning of the teacher so they can reposition the environment's affordances as a conduit to learning.

The practice architectures approach has influenced our approach to Pragmatic Adaptive Modelling. In the model we are developing in this book, though, we'd describe the finding we have just described slightly differently. We would say that we observed that simply the provision of different tools (the new environment) by the school to the teachers undertaking the activity of teaching did not result in different outcomes because the object of transformation (patterns of learning) was not itself adjusted. However, when the object of transformation was updated to nurture teachers' pedagogical reasoning, then the new tools became useful in causing a difference in the activity outcome (student learning).

Changing practices

One thing we have noticed in research using practice theory, including our own research, is a tendency to focus on the practice of just one actor or class of actors within a field. For example, in the case of the new STEM teaching environment we have just outlined, we have focused very much on the practices of the teacher. Figure 4.1b shows the relative proportion of time spent by the teacher on different practices related to teaching a class on 3D modelling. It is clear to see here that the teacher spent the greatest proportion of their time on sayings practices, and much less time on relatings practices. However, in doing this we have largely ignored the practices of the students. While the students' practices can be similarly mapped and analysed (Figure 4.1a), this approach makes it difficult for us to draw straight line relationships between the practices of the teacher and the corresponding practices of the students. In fact, a deeper understanding of the assumed interconnectivity of practices within the various forms of the theory suggests that such linear relationships are unlikely to be helpful and instead point to the necessity to consider those relationships through a lens of complexity.

In short, we have found that practice theories are both instrumental *and* insufficient to drive change, which has greatly impacted our research translation, where the ultimate goal is to support school leaders as they make critical decisions. Because of this, we need a framework that more directly supports practical and impactful intervention by representing the interactions of practices that occur simultaneously within a practice architecture. In our own work this has increasingly led to the use of Activity Theory, and particularly Engeström's work that led the so-called 'third generation' of this theory (Engeström, 1987).

Activity Theory

Activity Theory (AT), or more formally Cultural Historical Activity Theory (CHAT), has its origins in the Soviet psychology of Vygotsky, Luria and Leontiev. It is an interdisciplinary approach to studying human action that positions activity – the actual things that humans do – as the basic unit of analysis (Roth and Lee, 2007). In doing so, AT allows us to explore human work as something that is 'object-oriented'

THE COMPLEXITY OF LEARNING CONTEXTS

Figure 4.1: Observed teacher and student practices during a 3D modelling learning activity

(A) Student Practices: 3D Modelling   (B) Teacher Practices: 3D Modelling

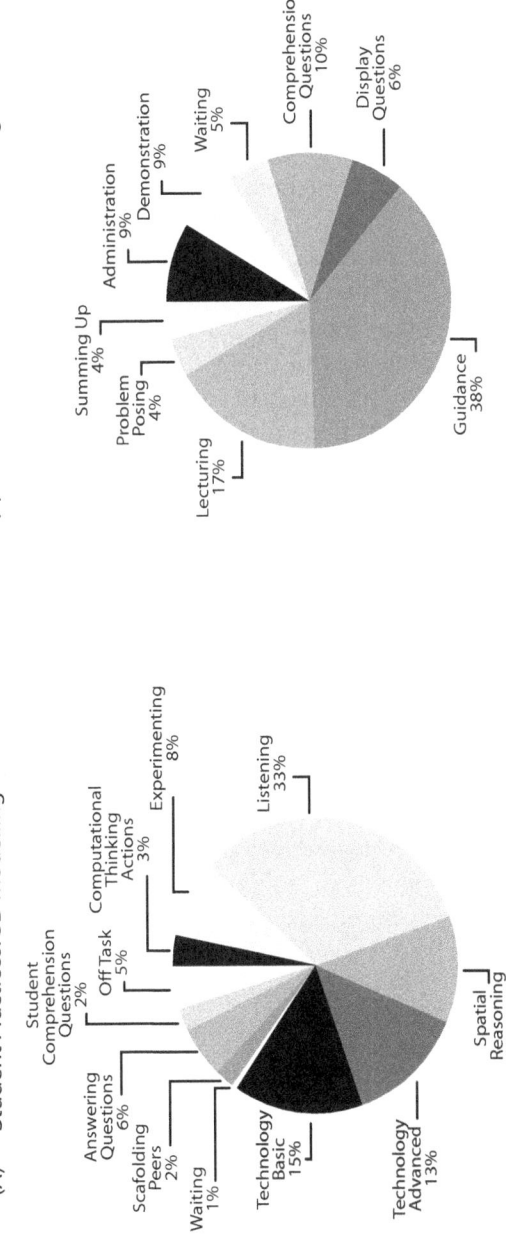

or purposeful, and which can also be driven by contradictions (Engeström, 1987; Yamagata-Lynch, 2010; Engeström and Sannino, 2021).

AT develops from the belief that human consciousness cannot be separated from context and purpose (Vygotsky et al, 1978). It provides a method for 'mapping' the interactions' consciousness, context and purpose (Engeström, 2006). We will discuss AT in much greater depth later in this chapter but, in short, AT considers an activity 'system' consisting of a 'subject' (person or group) doing work on an 'object' (a thing that is changed or transformed) while paying attention to the cultural and historical rules or norms, the tools available to do the work, the community in which the work is done, and how the tasks within that community of practice are divided.

The AT framework has proven a powerful way for understanding learning in context. Even its leading proponents (Engeström and Sannino, 2010; 2021), however, have acknowledged the limitations of AT – at least in its current form – in dealing with extremely complex activity such as where there are multiple activities doing work on the same object. Global scale 'wicked' problems such as climate change are often offered as examples of this kind of hyper-complex problem. In this context, a wicked problem can be a complex problem that is difficult to define and even more difficult to solve. Through our own research in the learning sciences, however, we would argue that the everyday work of schools also meets the criteria of a highly complex problem, and therefore a further generation of AT is needed to better cope with the interactions of the many activities of every school day. In search of such development, we have turned to theories of complexity.

Systems theory and complexity

We will say many times throughout this book that things may feel complicated, but they are really just complex.

Linear thinking follows simple equation-style solutions to big problems and assumes there are no variables that could affect this equation. In reality, any activity done by a human is actually done in a system, where there are a huge number of variables affecting an outcome. The word 'system' is often used colloquially to describe a variety of everyday phenomena, but here a system is defined as a collection of interrelated and/or interacting elements that function together towards a specific purpose or goal.

Systems have structures and processes defined by the relationships between elements, all of which dictates how the system behaves. From something as 'simple' as a clock, to huge, nebulous systems of government, there are often intangible 'rules' that define how these relationships occur. 'Systems thinking', on the other hand, is a way of viewing complex problems as an interconnected whole instead of as individual parts or elements. It emerged as a formal concept from the science and engineering advancements of the industrial revolution and is consequently often described in very mechanical terms. While elements in mechanical systems simply follow rules – if cog A turns this way, cog B will turn that way – systems that involve humans can be more volatile. Here, we realised, was a way of viewing activity and the goals of education in a more holistic way, instead of as a linear process.

In non-mechanical systems, elements that can make decisions about behaviour are called agents or subjects, while elements that describe things that can be used to achieve a goal we will refer to as resources or tools. Systems interact with their environment, such as how sunlight affects the ecosystem, or the curriculum affects what students learn in class, but the converse is not true. A system's environment both influences and provides controls and constraints to the system. A system can be described as being open – the system interacts with and exchanges resources such as energy, matter or information with its environment – or isolated – the system exchanges nothing with its environment. We can see here that all learning activity

Figure 4.2: A systems representation of a hypothetical science learning system and four simultaneous activity systems, some with unique objects of transformation, others with shared objects of transformation

a) A classroom system

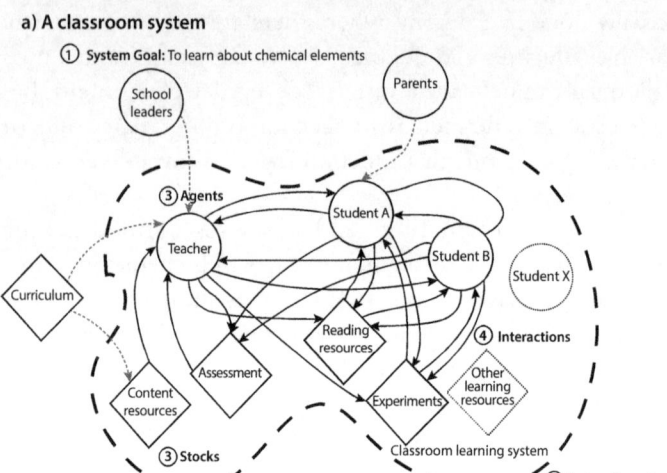

b) A classroom activity

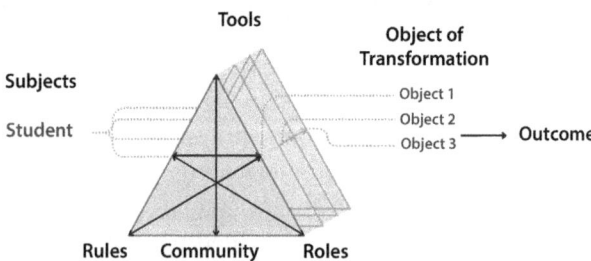

exists as an open system, where external variables affect what is happening in the activity.

To visualise this understanding, we can consider a 'classroom learning system' (Figure 4.2a). First, the goal of this system is defined as 'to learn about chemical elements', then the object of transformation would be a student's understanding of chemical elements. Here, the system boundary is drawn in a way that shows what is 'in' the activity, and it is comprised of a dotted line to show that it is an open, 'permeable' system. Next, we add the agents (circles) and tools/resources (diamonds) that we imagine are present in the system. In the case of our classroom example these are the learning resources, reference resources, teachers and students. We then know that all these elements have relationships with each other, and these are represented by lines. For example, the teacher may influence the reading resources to be used in the lesson, which in turn influences Student A's understanding of the topic. Student A is friends with Student B, and they choose to participate in the experiments together, influencing each other's behaviour. The arrows simply indicate the direction of influence, not the specific flow of materials or information. While these influences could be equal and opposite – in which case a double-headed arrow would be appropriate – it is more common for them to be unbalanced and hence drawn as two opposed arrows. For example, Student A might be more assertive that Student B, and so likely has a stronger directional influence on them than the other way round. Finally, we add other influences that exist outside of the system, which in our hypothetical situation might be influences from school leaders on teachers or parents on students.

Figure 4.2a is a rather contrived example of one aspect of a teacher's practice, yet even in this simple example, it is clear to see that the process of learning is much more complicated than simply 'filling students' heads with knowledge'.

Drawing systems like this can be extremely useful to show how many relationships occur but can also obscure the object and goals of an activity. Activity systems can be drawn alternatively as a triangle that 'categorises' the elements into tools, community, rules and divisions of labour, better capturing some of the invisible things that affect these relationships (Figure 4.2b). This form of system map highlights the object of transformation, giving some direction and purpose to the system, and so is useful for visualising deliberate activity. With this visualisation, we found a way to start looking at the big picture of problems that felt like runaway objects.

The classroom is really just a sub-system of a school, and there are many more systems occurring all at once to make up the 'Education System'. Systems engineers generally refer to these larger, more complicated structures as supersystems or systems of systems. In these, both agents and resources can exist simultaneously within multiple systems and can therefore be influenced by multiple systems goals at the same time. For example, a teacher in their classroom system may have the goal of imparting knowledge about chemical elements, at the same time as their principal is working to make the school a competitive sports hub. Indeed, within a system of systems, there is no requirement that the sub-system goals be compatible with each other, and it is likely that various reinforcing and balancing loops might naturally emerge from the system. This is where we clearly see that the neoliberal agenda of pumping out '*standardised workers*' could be in direct conflict with school activities focused on promoting student wellbeing and individuality. It is also entirely feasible for one sub-system to cause a change in another such that the nature of the interactions present changes. This adaptive property can lead to new emergent behaviours that are impossible to predict with any degree of certainty. It is at this point that we transition our thinking from a complicated system of systems approach to a truly complex adaptive system. This means we are often only seeing the tip of the iceberg, or what is immediately visible, when looking at just one activity, so it can be beneficial to map multiple interacting activities to explore these invisible overlaps.

In saying that, a key feature of systems and activities is that the interacting elements can cause unpredictable behaviours. Maybe the students learning chemical elements are completely distracted because they are thinking about the new, upcoming sports competition. Maybe the teacher diligently trying to teach chemistry just up and quits one day because they are burnt out from parent requests. Maybe the reading intervention that took a year to develop is seen as extremely old-fashioned by students because of a social media trend. All these examples show a system adaptation that requires us, as researchers and leaders, to be open and flexible to uncertainty.

There is a growing body of research across many fields that has sought to understand this unpredictability. Many of the early pioneers of complex adaptive systems (see Morowitz, 1994) focused on the idea of adaptive agents and the role that these systems might play in neurobiology, ecology and human behaviour. Others explored the ways in which complex adaptive systems could be used as a way of performing organisational diagnosis and to inform organisational (re-) design (for example, Viable Systems Model; Beer, 1984). Snowden (2005) built upon the idea of multiple observers contributing to the building of a complex system model through his Cynefin framework that provides opportunities for what he terms 'sensemaking'. Many of these approaches traditionally focused mainly on the physical and/or technical aspects of the systems they attempt to model; however, in recent years other researchers (for example, Kennedy et al, 2020) have begun to integrate methods that explore some of the soft systems or human factors aspects into the modelling process. Even though complex adaptive systems are still in an embryonic form within educational contexts, their use has started to gain some traction in recent years when dealing with wicked problems such as COVID-19 and managing school change.

This perspective on complexity is undoubtedly daunting. It would be reasonable to respond by asking, 'if everything is complex, how can we know anything or make any decisions?' The short answer is that in a complex world, the only certainty is uncertainty itself. Nevertheless, if we can discern the commonalities within all of these approaches to complex systems modelling then we can identify the key conceptual ingredients needed when exploring complex problems.

Fundamental to all approaches to modelling complex adaptive systems is the stark fact that they cannot be modelled completely. Researchers and leaders, therefore, need to be pragmatic when defining system boundaries so as to ensure that, although the models that will be produced will be wrong, they are at least useful. Secondly, systems are adaptive. This implies that whenever something is done *to* the system, there is a possibility that the system itself will change as a result and this extends to probing or measuring the system. This requires an iterative approach be adopted when working with the system: prod or otherwise provide a stimulus to the system, watch for changes, evaluate the observed changes, refine the model, and then prod the system again. Finally, we need to leverage many viewpoints if we are to build as complete a model of the system as possible. From a change design standpoint, it is therefore essential to spend sufficient time empathising with all relevant stakeholders to ensure that the problem and its system is defined well enough before providing the first prod.

The PAM approach that we describe next seeks to incorporate all these aspects when understanding complex education systems.

Pragmatic Adaptive Modelling

PAM is a dynamic, iterative approach to solving real-world problems, especially in complex systems like schools. The pitfall of much education research is that it exists within its own academic void and doesn't 'see the light of day' within an actual functioning school. Very often, we, as researchers, tend to design our tools and interventions for the ideal context but this does not stand up in the realistic chaos of an ordinary school day.

PAM bridges this gap by working directly with this subtle, everyday chaos to translate research into something that is contextually suitable. It involves continuously adjusting strategies and practices based on emerging behaviours and tensions within the activity system, instead of sticking to rigid, one-size-fits-all solutions, encouraging us to adapt to the specific needs and challenges that arise over time. This means that there aren't necessarily 'best practices' when it comes to employing solutions, but we are actively choosing to discover 'what works' in response to these complex system changes. Often, this will involve implementing many little tweaks and strategies over time, instead of one big change that is potentially unsustainable. Thankfully, it allows for real-time pragmatic adjustment in response to system change, which makes it a powerful framework for continuously improving complex, evolving systems.

Systems thinking is at the core of PAM. It is all about observing the system's behaviours and asking, 'what caused this?' and 'how can we push it this other way?' When we are modelling and responding to change, we find that referring to system maps is valuable for communicating or predicting what might happen in response to our intervention, but it also requires us to be personally flexible and experimental to keep up with the dynamics of the system.

A woolly example of Pragmatic Adaptive Modelling

Step 1: Futures Modelling and theories of change

To illustrate how to model an activity system, we will explore a simple system unrelated to education: the activity of sheep shearing. Let's imagine that Old MacDonald has a farm, and on that farm, he has a sheep ... and a problem. He has noticed that the farm is not meeting the daily sheep shearing quotas, but when he hired more shearers to help meet this quota, it was ineffective. He has always thought of his process as a simple 'black box' problem where the only limiting factor is the ratio of sheep to shearers, like in Figure 4.3. However, simply adjusting the input dials – that is, adjusting the ratio of

Figure 4.3: A black box process representation of the sheep shearing activity

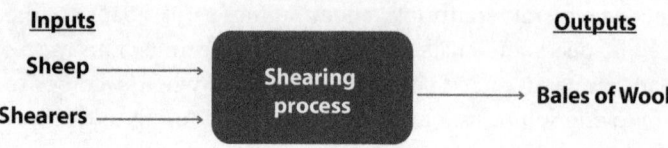

sheep to shearers – is not having the desired outcome effect. Old MacDonald now wants to work together with us to peer inside this black box and to solve this woolly problem. He invites us to use PAM to examine the internal problems that are occurring in the sheep shearing activity, and it becomes immediately evident that Old MacDonald doesn't have a simple problem – he has a complex one.

You don't have to know much about this activity to know that its purpose is to collect wool, but this is irrelevant without examining *why* we want to collect wool in the first place. Ultimately, we want to shear sheep because we want to make clothing, so woollen products can be seen as a long-term goal of the sheep shearing activity. To make sure the shearing fulfils this purpose, we can draw a theory of change to map out how we get from shearing to woollen products (Figure 4.4).

Step 2: Review risks and assumptions

In an ideal world, nothing goes wrong, and the production of woollen products thrives – but what if something does go wrong? What if not enough wool is collected? What if the processed wool never makes it to the factory? What if nobody is buying woollen products, so factories stop making woolly mittens? Old MacDonald's daily quotas will be determined by these factors.

These 'what ifs' can be written down as our assumptions and risks. An assumption is something that needs to occur for an outcome to eventuate, and the risk is something that prevents

Figure 4.4: Sheep shearing theory of change

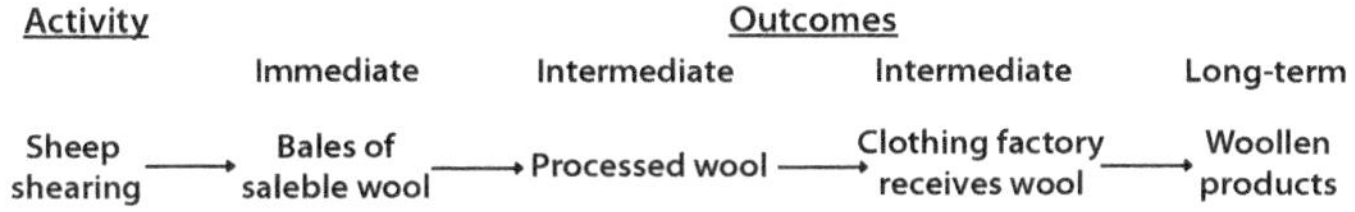

Activity	Outcomes			
	Immediate	Intermediate	Intermediate	Long-term
Sheep shearing →	Bales of saleable wool →	Processed wool →	Clothing factory receives wool →	Woollen products

the assumptions from coming true. When the likelihood of the assumptions being fulfilled outweighs the risks, the long-term outcome is more likely to succeed. These potential risks and assumptions of this woolly theory of change can be seen in Figure 4.5.

Now we can examine our theory of change to see if it makes sense. Does it logically follow that processed wool will make it to the factory? Only if the wool is of desirable quality, there is a market need for the wool and the shipping is successful. But there is a real risk that none of these things will happen, which could prevent wool making it to the factory and being made into woollen products. But some of these risks can actually be assessed to prevent downstream problems. For example, we can measure how much wool is damaged or of poor quality immediately after shearing, which will predict the quantity of saleable bales. We could then also measure how much marketing is happening to predict whether it will be sold to processors. We could also then assess the market need for wool to understand whether the clothing manufacturers will be buying the processed wool, which will affect how much wool the processors want to buy.

Now we have an understanding of where we want the wool to end up, and what might prevent it from getting there, we can start looking at whether we are doing the right activity in the first place. Is the market trending towards cashmere instead of sheep wool? Maybe our sheep shearing activity is inappropriate for the long-term goal.

But let's say the market wants woollen products, and our theory of change logically gets us to the long-term goal. Now we can look at the actual activity that is occurring.

Figure 4.5: Woollen products assumptions and risks

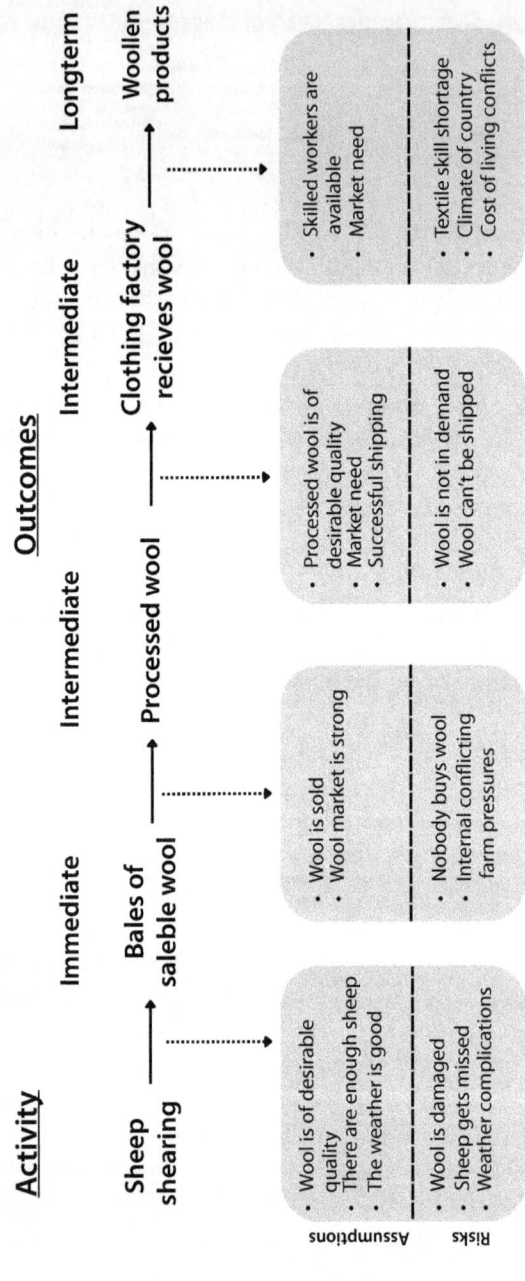

Step 3: Examine the activity system through Situational Mapping

Situational Mapping describes what is currently happening in the activity. This step is essentially the same process as undertaking an Activity Systems Analysis using the approach of third generation Activity Theory (Yamagata-Lynch, 2010).

Often, when we are planning designs and implementations, we will be tempted to design for the hypothetical ideal. That is, we will be tempted to assume that all aspects of a system are as they first appear to be, and we may overlook those things that are '*off*'. Situational Mapping can be thought of as empathising with the activity, so it is important to incorporate the differing perspectives of many stakeholders when constructing the overall situational map or activity system. Usually, Situational Mapping will happen as part of the initial problem analysis phase of a Design-Based Research cycle (McKenney and Reeves, 2013), where we collect quantitative and qualitative data to inform what the activity looks like. An activity system of a sheep shearing activity might look like Figure 4.6.

In this activity the things being changed (the object of transformation) are the fibres that keep the wool attached to the sheep. If our activity is successful, we will remove the sheep from the wool we want, and we will end up with a shorn sheep and some unattached wool. Here, the amount of wool is an observable measure of the system's success, and even though the shorn sheep is a by-product of the activity, we can estimate how much wool we have gathered if we count the shorn sheep, too (without falling asleep).

The subject in this system is the person enacting the activity, which is the shearer. How does the shearer get the wool off the sheep? With tools. In this activity the tools are clippers, the shed and shoes that maintain grip, all of which are making the activity more efficient.

Looking at just the shearer, the sheep/wool and the tools is insufficient to show the full complexities of the system,

Figure 4.6: Situational map of sheep shearing activity

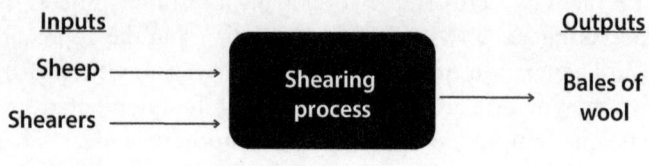

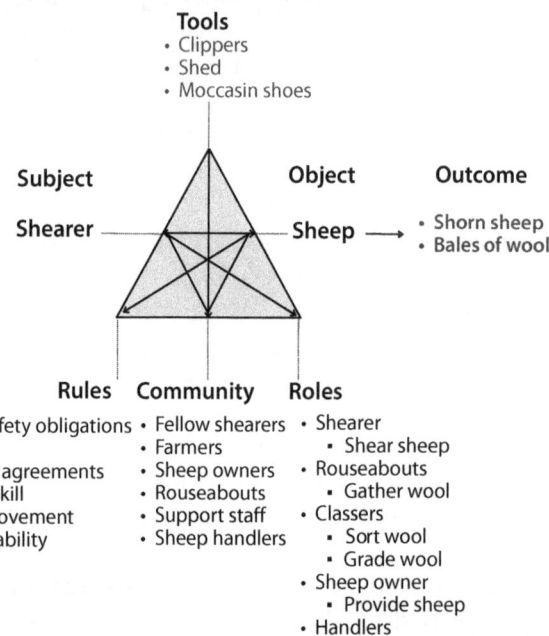

so we need to investigate who else is contributing to the activity and supporting the shearing. We can see here that the community consists of fellow shearers, farmers and sheep owners, rouseabouts (wool gatherers) and sheep handlers.

They all have their own roles and responsibilities that affect the success of the shearing activity and where if a role isn't performed, the activity will yield less wool at the end.

But any time people are involved in doing anything, there will be implicit and explicit social norms or constraints that affect how people behave. Some of the social norms, or rules, that affect the sheep shearing activity might be sheep safety obligations, how much time is available for shearing, or the shearers' initial skill and physical ability.

Now that we have a simple map of the system, we can investigate how these elements interact internally, or towards the long-term goal.

Step 4: Collect data about the invisible system elements

What we have presented is the hypothetical ideal of the sheep shearing system, where all the tools, rules and division of labour are working together to produce lots of high-quality wool. However, Old MacDonald approached us precisely because something in this system wasn't working as efficiently as he hoped for. This is where we can map the invisible elements of the system to see what is going on below the surface.

To understand the actual system, we can conduct a Situational Analysis, also known as Situational Mapping. This is a process of data collection to understand the finer points of the activity. How this data is collected is contingent on the activity, but can involve quantitative or qualitative data collection or, ideally, both.

On Old MacDonald's farm, let us imagine that we have collected qualitative data about the wool collection and quality, observed the process of sheep shearing, conducted interviews with the community of practice in this activity, and found some key themes:

- The shearers were highly experienced and passionate about their work.
- Old MacDonald had recently updated the shearing tools.

- There was a strong market need for wool.
- The sheep were rowdy and energetic.
- The shearing shed was inefficient.
- The weather had been poor recently.
- The shearers believed other farm workers were working inefficiently.

With this data, we could then map the situation at Old MacDonald's farm to find enablers and tensions in the activity.

Step 5: Identify enablers

Enablers are interactions between system elements that help the activity succeed. These may be useful tools, supportive relationships, clear guidelines and relevant skills. Identifying these enablers means looking at which resources and dynamics make the process effective, so they can be strengthened to boost overall performance and adaptability. We draw lines between the elements that interact and enable the outcome. Dotted lines denote relationships that enable the activity, and we have labelled them for clarity in Figure 4.7.

We found there were three clear enablers in the system:

- Enabler A: The shearers were highly skilled and able to quickly and efficiently shear the sheep, so skill level enabled completion rates.
- Enabler B: Shearers and farms hands reported that they had all the tools needed complete their jobs.
- Enabler C: There was a strong market need for wool, and this need was predicted to remain strong. This enabled Old MacDonald to establish realistic shearing quotas for the shearers to meet.

Seeing so many enablers is optimistic, and yet, Old MacDonald still reported that the shearing quotas weren't being met. Clearly, something else was going on, which is why his linear

Figure 4.7: Enablers of sheep shearing activity

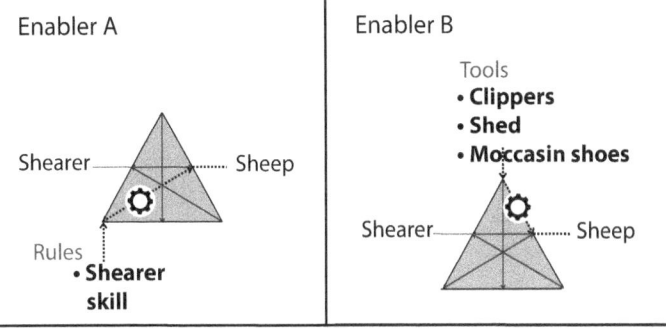

Note: Cogs represent enablers

solution of hiring more shearers wasn't working. This comes down to tensions, which are relationships that slow down – or completely inhibit – the activity's success.

Step 6: Identify tensions

The process of tension modelling allows us to consider the complex realities of the activity system and to address any hidden barriers and unidentified risks. This modelling can be carried out through observation and/or by engaging with different community members or role bearers to obtain their experience of the activity as viewed from their perspective. By overlaying these differing perspectives, we as researchers can identify aspects of dissonance or conflict and ensure that those are accurately captured in our activity system. Some simple questions to get you started are:

- Are the tools adequate for the job?
- Are tasks clearly delineated, or is there confusion about who does what?
- Are there formal or informal rules that contradict each other or that are hard to follow?
- Do people work well together, or is there friction?
- Do people agree on the purpose and outcome of the activity?
- How do we know we are moving towards our long-term goal?
- Are there activities in the future that undermine the current activity?

We have modelled these tensions as dashed lines and labelled them for easy identification (Figure 4.8).

These tensions may not be apparent without data to back them up, but for the sake of this analogy let us imagine we made suitable observations when examining the shearing activities.

- Tension A: Usually, the shearing shed is set up to facilitate the sheep shearing, but we saw that the shed actually had an inappropriate layout, so people were getting in each other's way, creating a tension where this tool wasn't actually an effective tool at all.
- Tension B: The next tension we saw was that there were internal conflicts elsewhere on the farm, which slowed down shearing. This, in turn, was affecting Old MacDonald's motivation to participate in the community.
- Tension C: Then we saw that the sheep were acting erratically instead of predictably, which was making it difficult to safely shear them, so the shearers had to choose between their obligations to keep the sheep safe and their time constraints. This movement was also slowing down the rouseabouts who were having trouble gathering wool before it got trampled, exacerbating the risk of damaged wool.

Figure 4.8: Tensions in sheep shearing activity

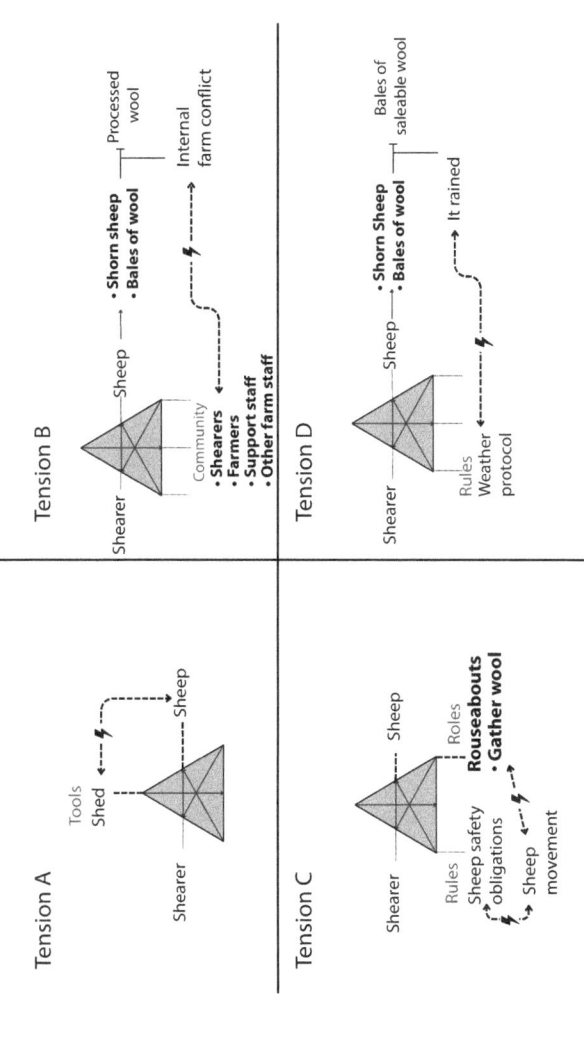

Note: Dashed lines highlight the tensions in the system

- Tension D: Finally, it was a rainy week, and there were inadequate wet-weather protocols in place. As a consequence, the slippery sheep were hard to safely shear, and the wool was rain-damaged. In fact, it could be that the rain is causing the erratic behaviour, and the inefficient shed (A) is creating a bottleneck that normally goes unnoticed.

Situation mapping can go on to reveal many tiny interactions, but we have chosen these four as the main, or most impactful, tensions. Breaking them down in this way can help us identify practical design solutions.

Step 7: Identify actionable solutions that unravel tensions

During situational mapping, we found quite different tensions, which means there isn't one single solution to all these problems. Instead, imagine that Old MacDonald approached us to ideate some key decisions towards change.

We can break these down as follows:

Tension A: Inefficient shed
Problem: Is the shed the right tool for the job?
Solution: Use a different shed on the farm that is more efficient.
Solution: Redesign the inside of the shed.
Tension B: Internal farm conflicts
Problem: How to alleviate these internal conflicts?
Solution: Map the situation of the whole farm.
Tension C: Sheep are rowdy and unsafe
Problem: How do we maximise sheep safety?
Solution: Structure the shed so sheep can move without hazards.
Solution: Leverage enabler B (highly skilled shearers) for design solution ideas.
Problem: How to minimise sheep movement?
Solution: Structure the shed so sheep can move efficiently.
Solution: Use dogs to more efficiently to manage sheep behaviour.

Tension D: It rained
Problem: How to we mitigate the problems with rain?
Solution: Evaluate rain protocols.
Solution: Provide shearers and handlers with rain-safety training.

Sheep shearing is a relatively simple activity compared to a school, but we can already see how many complex factors are actually affecting the activity and eventual long-term outcomes for Old Macdonald's farm. However, PAM helps us identify and articulate these many complexities that are highly specific to Old Macdonald's context, so the solutions can be specifically tailored to his needs.

Futures Modelling: parallel, simultaneous and symbiotic relationships

Futures Modelling allows us to look beyond a single activity and examine how multiple systems are working towards a shared goal or (complex) outcome. In the previous examples, we still have the problem of Tension B – something else is going on at Old Macdonald's farm that is affecting the success of sheep shearing. As noted earlier, systems can affect each other and interactions are rarely of equal strength, so it's pragmatic to look at how interactions between systems can also lead to tensions.

In addition to the sheep, Old Macdonald had a wheat crop that needed to be kept healthy, which is an altogether different activity. However, as the two activities are both being carried out on the same farm, they function in parallel. They can be thought of as two sub-systems within the larger complicated farm system.

Returning to the Situational Analysis, imagine that we collected more data and found the following tensions (Figure 4.9).

- Tension A: The sheep paddock was too close to the wheat field and the herbicide spray disturbed the sheep, making them rowdy all month.

Figure 4.9: Tensions between the parallel activities of sheep shearing and crop management on Old MacDonald's farm

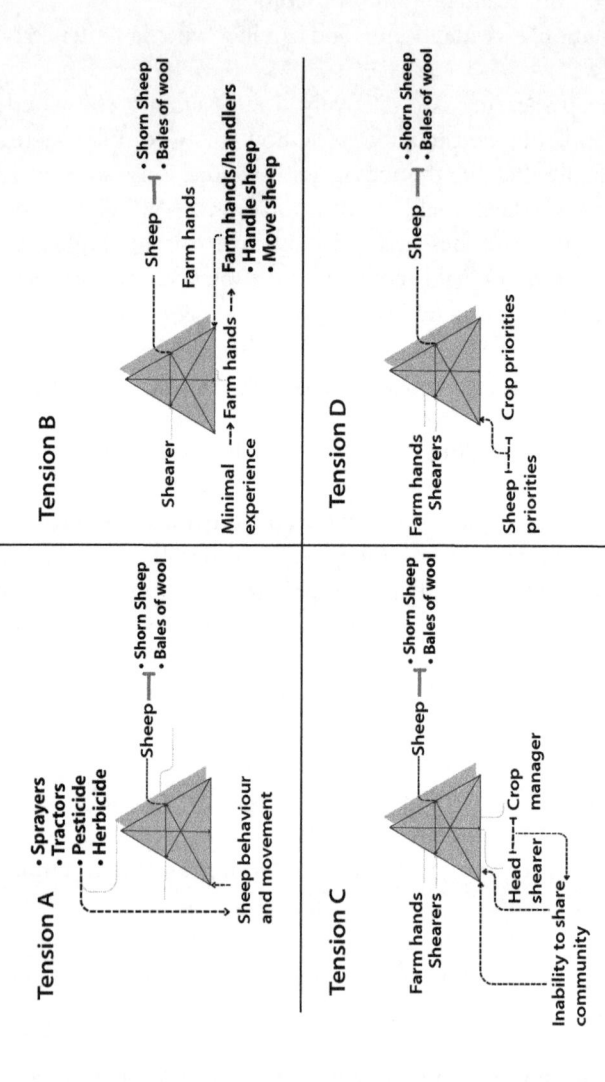

- Tension B: They were unable to spray the crops due to the rain, so more farm hands were able to be released to act as rouseabouts. This meant that there were more rouseabouts in the shed performing their role. The extra farm hands were mostly unskilled but enthusiastic and so were constantly getting in the way of each other and other community members in the shearing shed and making mistakes.
- Tension C: The Crop Manager and Head Shearer had had a personal conflict and avoided each other, creating a culture that prevented both communities coming together. Because neither was able to see how this affected their own activity, a shared social norm of not working together became established, and the farm hands were never properly trained as rouseabouts.
- Tension D: Amidst this personal conflict, both communities were obliged to prioritise their own activities, so it ultimately came down to Old MacDonald to choose the farm's top priority. It is also clear here that long-term goals of the wool activity are irrelevant to the crop management activity, so it might be wise to re-examine the theory of change. Instead, Old MacDonald may realise that his actual long-term goal is to make lots of money – a goal that both the shearers and crop managers can agree with.

Adding complexity

Already we can see that the outcomes of the shearing activity were deeply affected by the crop management system, and probably vice versa, and that there were dependent links between the shearing activity and the classing activity. We must, therefore, make use of Futures Modelling to consider all the systems on the farm as a single complex ecology of linked sub-systems if we are to gain insight into what is really going on. Without this, it is far too easy to miss the deeper explanations for why Old MacDonald's goals aren't being met.

Pragmatic Adaptive Modelling and systems modelling

Earlier in this chapter, we described systems as being composed of interrelated and interacting elements (agents and resources) working together to achieve a given goal within a defined system boundary. The PAM approach is an alternative visualisation. Tools generally represent resources in the system while subjects, rules, communities and roles can be thought of loosely as agents. Where PAM differs somewhat is in the addition of an explicit object of transformation. This can be thought of as a flow of *something* in from the environment that is changed by the system and that then flows out again. All PAM representations are thus open systems and are always part of something larger and more complicated. If we therefore consider each of the sub-systems of a complex system to be its own PAM, then the inter-system interactions will themselves form their own super-activity systems.

Taken to the extreme, we will end up back where we started with a system that is far too complex to understand. However, the processes of enabler identification and situation mapping that we have highlighted here provide a pragmatic way to identify those areas of the system where we are most likely to find wool that we can spin into gold and enable system change.

Conclusion

In this chapter we have introduced some of the theory underpinning the PAL approach. Each theoretical approach we have introduced clearly has value in leading and researching education, but each has its own set of limitations, too. We have then outlined how PAM, within the PAL framework, can address some of those limitations.

The PAM approach to modelling has been introduced using a rather abstract agricultural analogy, so, in the next chapter, we will return to educational concerns. More specifically, the next chapter will begin to explore what we see as the 'future-oriented' concerns of contemporary educational policy and research.

FIVE

Pragmatic Adaptive Modelling: expanding the educational world

Corroboree Frog College as a case study

Building on our explanation of Pragmatic Adaptive Modelling (PAM) in the previous chapter, this chapter presents a case study demonstrating how we applied PAM in a real-life educational context through an ongoing university–school partnership with Corroboree Frog College (CFC). This collaboration aimed to address the complexities of preparing students to thrive beyond school. As we undertook this journey, we navigated many different aspects of the college and its unique context, but the most exciting part of the story is seeing new leadership emerge within the college itself. This was a highlight of the work – but let us start at the beginning to show how we got there.

Contextualising the school

Like most schools, CFC wanted to develop students who would thrive as active citizens in their post-school life. This was already in line with our ultimate goals, but it was clear from the beginning that our team and the CFC team were coming from vastly different backgrounds. We both knew where we wanted to get to, but we weren't sure of how to get there. Yet, with our partnership formed, and with a shared long-term goal in mind, we set about the arduous task of attempting to effect change.

Unsurprisingly, there were a plethora of cultural norms and nuances that were unique to CFC. It was evident from the very beginning of our partnership that the staff predominantly cared deeply about their students' futures, which is a powerful enabler to help students thrive post-school. But, again, like most schools constrained by the pressure of neoliberal metrics of success, CFC also had a deep culture and history that was resistant to changing practices. In the language of systems thinking, we might say that CFC demonstrated significant systemic inertia and resilience.

To bring us all onto the same page, we collaborated on developing a shared theory of change with the current CFC leadership. We began by imagining a hypothetical student who will eventually go on to do great things in life – let's call her Winnie. Winnie could be any student in any school. She represents a young learner full of potential; someone who is eager to explore the world around her, solve problems and make a difference in the future, but she is also juggling the complexities of growing up in a turbulent world. Winnie embodies the qualities of many students, with the capacity to grow, adapt and eventually achieve great things, no matter her starting point. Like all students, she will have her own interests, abilities, cultural context and life out of school, so you may choose to think of a child in your life who can be embodied in our hypothetical Winnie. In this narrative, Winnie's purpose is to remind us that all subjects in an activity system are human beings whose lives and futures matter. This empathy is central to the Design Thinking process, which we will expand upon in the next chapter, but it ultimately allows us to imagine Winnie as a real person, and to ask the question: how do we help her thrive in life?

Contextualising the student

For Winnie to thrive in her post-school life, we must see her as both a product of the 'now' and as the protagonist of many different futures. While it is common for schools to share and voice this lofty and worthy goal, in reality, the average school has very little data about their former students' post-secondary life. As such, it isn't always clear whether the tools used to develop students like Winnie are effective beyond the end of their time in formal education. It is also important to acknowledge here that while Winnie may be the subject of many activity systems within the wider school system, with respect to the system as a whole Winnie is the object of transformation. Therefore, once our changed Winnie flows out through the system boundary, the system ceases to be able to exert any further direct influence on her.

This absence of future data means that the only metrics we can use to infer future success are those that are embedded within the school system, where the cultural expectations of success are, in practice, often directly tied to academic success (Biesta, 2010). This is further exacerbated by myriad other stakeholder needs – such as needing to clearly articulate student progress to parents, obligations to perform in state and federal standardised testing, and curriculum priorities – which may lie within the system boundaries or within its environment.

In response to this, much of education is driven towards getting Winnie to graduation, potentially with a specific grade score average or set of behaviours or embodying a set of graduate qualities. It's clearly not for lack of good will, but the systemic pressures are so strong that taking a complex, futures-focused view of success is, frankly, so difficult that it's often ignored. This challenge is even more difficult to navigate if the end goal isn't mapped onto a well understood theory of change, because there are no defined or measurable steps that accurately indicate Winnie is on the right trajectory, or that she has the right support systems in place to become a competent, agentic adult in a changing world. That is, we haven't actually defined the waypoints to know if Winnie is on the way to becoming a thriving active citizen of her post-school world or not. The reality is, no matter what we change about Winnie's activity system today, there is a risk that it may be ineffective at overcoming current system tensions or inevitable future system change. It may feel like an impossible problem, but it is really just complex.

As initially understood, Winnie's school learning activity system looked like Figure 5.1.

The first thing we noticed during this modelling exercise was a number of major assumptions present in this theory of change. Overall, it assumed that academic ability led to success in post-secondary education. This in and of itself is not overly surprising given the neoliberal-informed approach to high stakes testing and to knowledge acquisition. However, there are clear risks that other personal and external pressures – such as personality, inequity and financial constraints – could prevent success in post-secondary education, regardless of academic ability and success at school (Li and Carroll, 2020; Ball et al, 2024). The second assumption was that success in post-secondary education was driven by high conceptual understanding, instead of a complex network of overlapping skills and capabilities needed to navigate the changing nature of the 21st century (Dishon and Gilead, 2021). That is, it was assumed that the object of transformation for Winnie's learning activity system was *just* her conceptual understanding. A third assumption was that Winnie would be able to transfer her 21st-century skills – which are often skewed towards labour skills – to other aspects of her life. This third assumption is particularly interesting, as although CFC itself makes it explicit that success in post-secondary life reaches beyond the idea of career, it is clear that the concept of career still holds an implicit societal value that exists in the environment beyond the education system. The final assumption was that this representation was sufficient in explaining what Winnie's actual activity looked like at school.

PRAGMATIC ADAPTIVE MODELLING

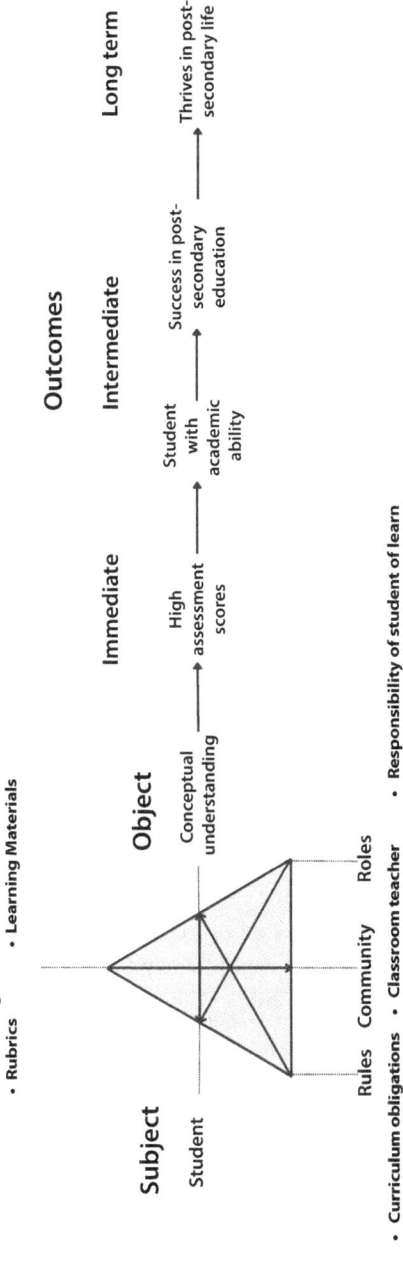

Figure 5.1: Traditional view of a learning activity system

Amidst all these assumptions, it became clear that we needed to collaboratively map the current system and ultimately create a new theory of change. This would provide leadership with a clear, shared vision for the entire school to aim for. In the ideal world, we may have created a theory of change before we began a project; but, like many projects in the real world, we needed to work with a complex system that was currently already in operation. So, while we looked to the future, we also had to recognise the present.

Enriching the picture

At this time, we were early in our partnership, and needed to gather data that would allow us to best represent Winnie's activity system before identifying the enablers and tensions that impeded Winnie and her peers from thriving in life. We suspected that academic achievement alone would be insufficient to enable Winnie's post-school success, and so we drew on two data collection instruments to understand students at a more holistic level.

The first instrument was the Student Attitude Survey (SAS), which we adapted to collect a measure of students' attitudes towards their learning areas (Kennedy et al, 2016). In this conception, school attitudes are a multidimensional measure of students' affective dispositions towards their formal learning experiences. The SAS measures nine attitudinal factors for each learning area: perceived difficulty, subject anxiety, lesson enjoyableness, self-efficacy, subject relevance, subject usefulness (for career), subject usefulness (for personal life), creative potential, and intentions to continue study in each subject area. Of particular interest to our discussion of Winnie will be her self-efficacy and her subject anxiety.

The SAS is an unusual instrument in a number of ways. First, it can be used to produce a snapshot profile of students at a given point in time across nine attitudinal dimensions and across all of a student's learning areas. This allows for potential 'hotspots' to be identified (Figure 5.2) and for sources of tension or enablement to be identified. Second, the SAS reports results using a relative scale known as their composite score. This allows for recognition of the realities of the student's present level of performance to be considered while avoiding the need to place value meanings on any specific value. For example, consider a situation where both Winnie and Lucy report self-efficacy scores for English of ten points. Does this mean that Winnie and Lucy have equal self-efficacy in English? Maybe? Maybe not? If Winnie had an average self-efficacy, a composite self-efficacy, score of 20 points, then we would know that Winnie feels less self-efficacious in English than in most other subjects. Similarly, if Lucy's composite self-efficacy score were -30 points, then we would know she felt much more self-efficacious in English than in her other subjects. For Winnie, the role she might have to play in English could be a source of tension in her learning system, while for Lucy, it might be an enabling influence. Finally, the SAS was designed to be used as a longitudinal instrument. On second and subsequent uses, the instrument is initialised to that student's previous levels and not to zero. This results in the SAS naturally capturing the *change* in attitudes over time and in response to stimuli and absolute meaning of individual levels becomes far less important to the understanding of the system.

How is this information useful in understanding the activity of education? By considering Winnie's attitudes towards her school subjects (Figure 5.2), it becomes immediately obvious that Winnie holds different attitudes about different subject areas. Furthermore, her subject profiles (the rows) and the attitude profiles (the columns) reveal different patterns in different areas. The implication from this is that a single model of Winnie's learning activity will show that she makes use of different tools, rules and roles in different classes and when operating on different objects of transformation. For example, should her mathematics teacher offer her learning experiences that can leverage her self-efficacy as an effective tool then

Figure 5.2: School Attitudes Survey hotspot map for Winnie

	Self-efficacy	Enjoyability	Career usefulness	Anti-anxiety	Non-difficulty	Creativity	Personal usefulness	Relevance	Intentions
English	-1.17	-4.83	10.50	-1.00	-6.22	-8.44	17.11	-3.61	18.78
Mathematics	21.83	20.17	23.50	14.00	4.78	10.56	6.11	22.39	24.78
Sciences	8.83	4.17	14.50	6.00	-5.22	-0.44	18.11	12.39	21.78
Humanities and social sciences	-1.67	-1.33	-37.00	0.00	-0.22	-7.44	-2.89	-7.11	-16.22
Creative and performing arts	-13.17	-10.83	-42.50	-12.00	-6.22	-3.44	-35.89	-23.61	-41.22
Technology and applied studies	5.83	13.17	7.50	6.00	6.78	6.56	-2.89	13.39	12.78
Health and physical education	-22.17	-37.83	28.50	-33.00	4.78	-16.44	-17.89	-29.61	-38.22
Languages other than English	-15.17	-27.83	-46.50	-22.00	-11.22	-27.44	-40.89	-35.61	-41.22
Composite score	13.00	4.70	-7.20	8.00	37.20	2.70	-9.40	-2.10	-10.40

Shading key: Relative strength / Strength / Neutral / Weakness / Relative weakness

Note: Bolder text indicates stronger impacts. White text indicates areas of weakness while black text indicates areas of strength. Traffic light colour was used in the original representation.

it is likely that Winnie will experience a degree of success. However, should her French teacher ask Winnie to complete a similar learning task, then it would be understandable if we observed different outcomes or different internal activity given her much lower level of self-efficacy in this subject.

Similar displays were also created that show the attitudes of cohorts of students varied across CFC (Figure 5.3). While a display such as this is far too dense to be useful for extracting specific data, it does allow us to observe potential patterns that can inform how we view the overall activity of education at CFC. For example, we can see that across many attitudinal factors, students responded in a very narrow range for both humanities and science. This indicates that making a uniform change to activity systems involving these subject areas will likely result in perceptible differences to outcomes. However, some subject areas, such as mathematics or health and physical education, exhibit much wider ranging attitudes across the

Figure 5.3: A cross-cohort look at School Attitudes Survey data for Winnie's peers at Corroboree Frog College

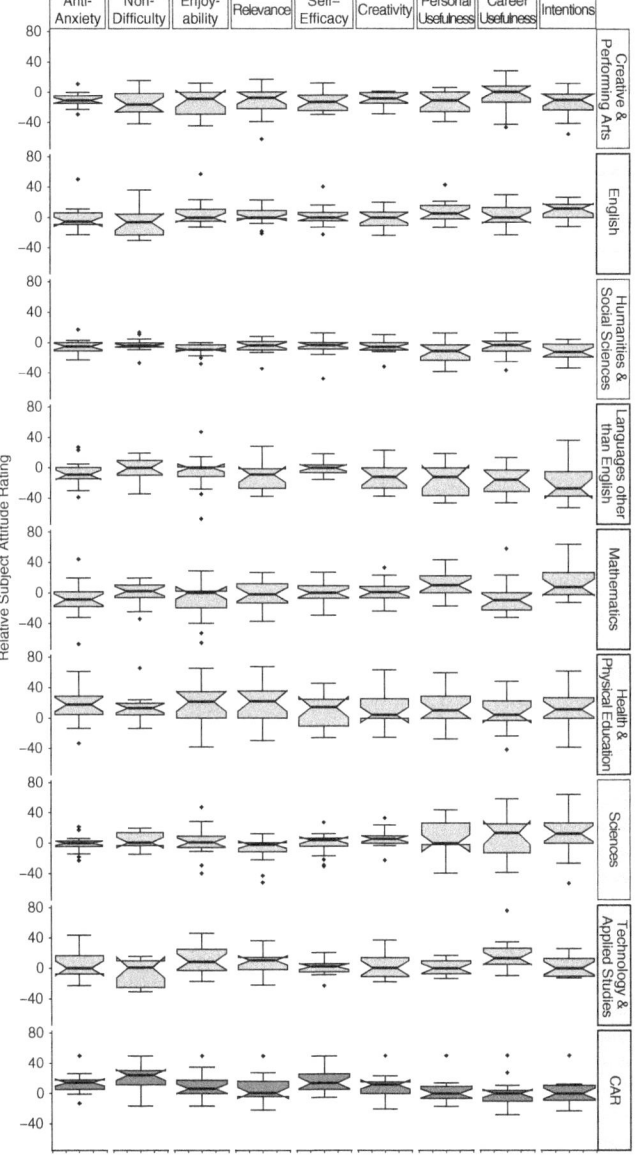

cohort. In these cases, we need to be aware that changes we make may benefit some students while restricting others; that is, we may inadvertently create unforeseen tensions in the system.

Since embarking on this collaboration with CFC we have monitored students' attitudes towards their school subjects four times per year and we have been able to track students in some cases over a five-year period (so far). What we have seen is that, on average, students' overall attitudes towards school tend to change very slowly, if at all. However, the internal structure of attitude ratings within an individual student's profile is constantly subject to ebb and flow over time. This individual internal variation can often be masked by the 'noise' of the cohort and could result in the prescription of a treatment that would benefit the average student; unfortunately, such a treatment would be doomed to fail simply because no individual student actually aligns with this average student.

It also became apparent from the whole school picture that the students as a whole hold very different attitudes towards different subjects at school. Ultimately, this has provided further evidence that our picture of Winnie's learning activity system as outlined earlier is incomplete and it has reinforced our commitment to work with the teachers at CFC to develop tightly focused and well-defined changes to the way they practice teaching and learning.

Wellness and Engagement Collection

The second data collection instrument we drew from was the South Australia Wellbeing and Engagement Collection (WEC) survey (Gregory and Brinkman, 2020), which collects information about a broad range of non-academic factors that might affect learning. This information is mapped to one of four domains: emotional wellbeing, engagement with school, learning readiness, and health and wellbeing out of school. The WEC is administered to students in Years 4 to 12 during the first half of each year and reports are shared with the school later in the year with the intent of assisting in reviewing, planning and decision making. Only summary data on a year-by-year basis is readily available to school leaders, making it somewhat difficult for these data to inform practice. Adding further challenge to interpreting the data is the fact that the WEC was designed to be an instrument that is very sensitive to low levels of wellbeing. Hence, in 'normal' contexts results tend to be skewed towards the high wellbeing end of the scale and are not normally distributed. Schools participate in the WEC on a voluntary basis and are under no obligation to participate.

We know that student wellbeing plays an enormous part in moderating the effectiveness of learning activity systems even though it may often be taken for granted and overlooked when formulating a traditional activity system such as Winnie's. As the WEC data was available to us, we thought it was prudent to explore the data and to try adding this to our rich understanding of learning at CFC.

Although the summary data are only available in cross-sectional form, we were able to stitch together multiple years of data to reverse engineer a composite data set. We were able to use this in such a way that we could infer how some of the different aspects of wellbeing might vary across CFC and as the students developed. A sample of these analyses are shown in Figure 5.4 for four of the WEC measures. These data are similar of those available to the leaders at CFC but have been adjusted in terms of scale and format for the purposes of discussion here.

What we found was that for most aspects of wellbeing, the proportion of students reporting high levels of wellbeing declined as they got older. This is in keeping with what researchers know about adolescent development. However, the data show that not all patterns were the same for all groups of students. For example, both male and female students reported similar, linear declines in cognitive engagement between Year 4 and Year 10. Yet, while female students showed a significant non-linear decline in emotion regulation over time, their male peers experienced a much more subtle and gradual decline. It

Figure 5.4: A sample of some Wellbeing and Engagement Collection trends across time

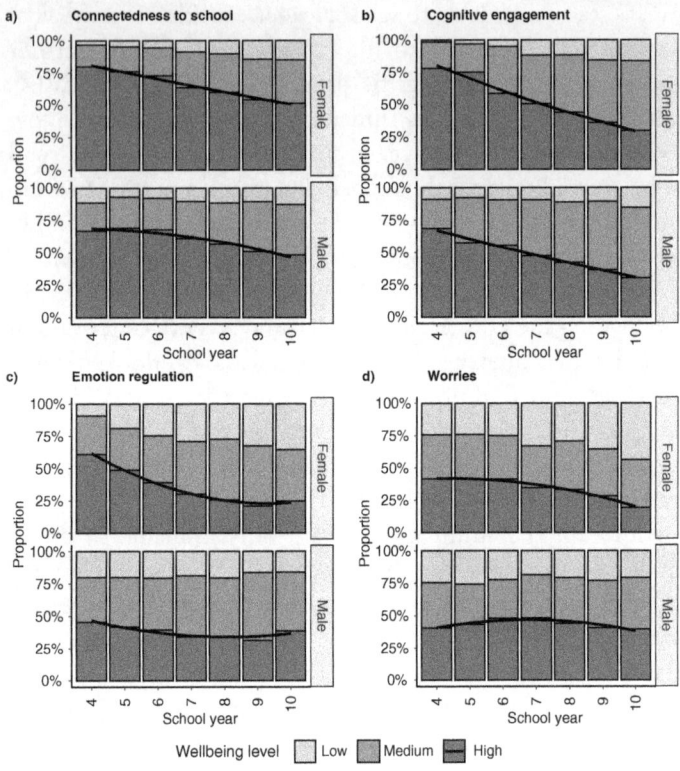

must be noted in this case, however, that the male students had much lower levels of high emotion regulation to begin with. While we were able to describe the patterns of wellbeing across the school and we can know what is going on at a single point in time from a cohort perspective, we are unable to use the school's WEC data to answer two critical questions: what is the 'typical' or expected pattern of wellbeing development? And what is happening with Winnie's wellbeing?

The first of these is particularly problematic from a pragmatic leadership perspective as without this information it is very difficult to allocate resources efficiently. To address this question, we utilised publicly available summary data collected from a seven-year period to create models that describe the typical changes in student wellbeing as students get older. These typical trajectories are shown as dotted lines in Figure 5.5 overlaid on the CFC data. As the statewide data are only available without gender information, the CFC data had to be merged for the comparisons to be useful. This new representation revealed that while the trajectories for some areas follow the statewide typical patterns of development, those for other areas were different. For example, we can see that students report higher levels of cognitive engagement for longer at CFC than might typically be expected. We can also see that if we feel we need to address declining cognitive engagement then that intervention needs to happen early in a student's school life before the observed decline becomes too steep. However, while providing actionable insights into the nature of the wellbeing trajectories seen at CFC, these additional data remain unable to explain *why* things are different.

Quantitative data like that obtained using the WEC or the SAS are extremely valuable because they highlight subtle trends and allow us to see what is going on over time and in response to various stimuli. However, they still only show a 'surface level' picture of what is actually happening. To understand these trends, we need to ask deeper questions: How has a trend changed? What do people perceive to have been the cause of the change? What might this be telling us about the larger system? To really understand these trends, we need to draw a map of existing tensions.

Situational Mapping: applying SAS and WEC

The ongoing SAS and WEC data collection provided us with an interesting perspective on the students' activity systems. If we think of Winnie again, we can clearly see that she does not exist in a vacuum; she is engaged in multiple,

Figure 5.5: Some Wellbeing and Engagement Collection trends across time as seen at Corroboree Frog College and the typical development of these factors by school year

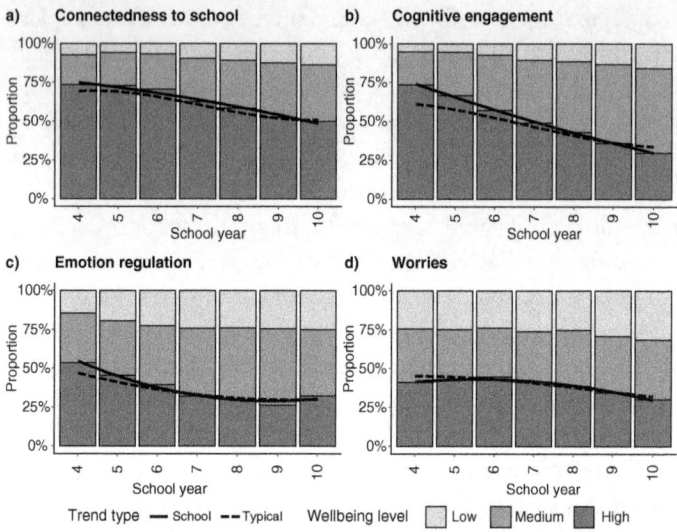

simultaneous systems of activity that interact with each other in both enabling and tensioning relationships. Elements of one system – for example, the rules related to group work utilised in a learning activity focused on improving conceptual understanding – may be in tension with, or enabled by, elements in another system that Winnie is engaged with – for example the tools related to self-regulated learning. Likewise, there may be feedback loops between her 'wellbeing' activity and her 'conceptual understanding' activity, where one fundamentally undermines the other. Looking through the lens of SoLD, Winnie's ideal theory of change could be more like Figure 5.6.

Now we have reached a point where we can begin to look at how system elements react, especially if those relationships cause useful – or even harmful – tensions, enablers and feedback loops. When one activity influences another, and vice versa,

Figure 5.6: Modelling a student's simultaneous activity systems and future trajectory

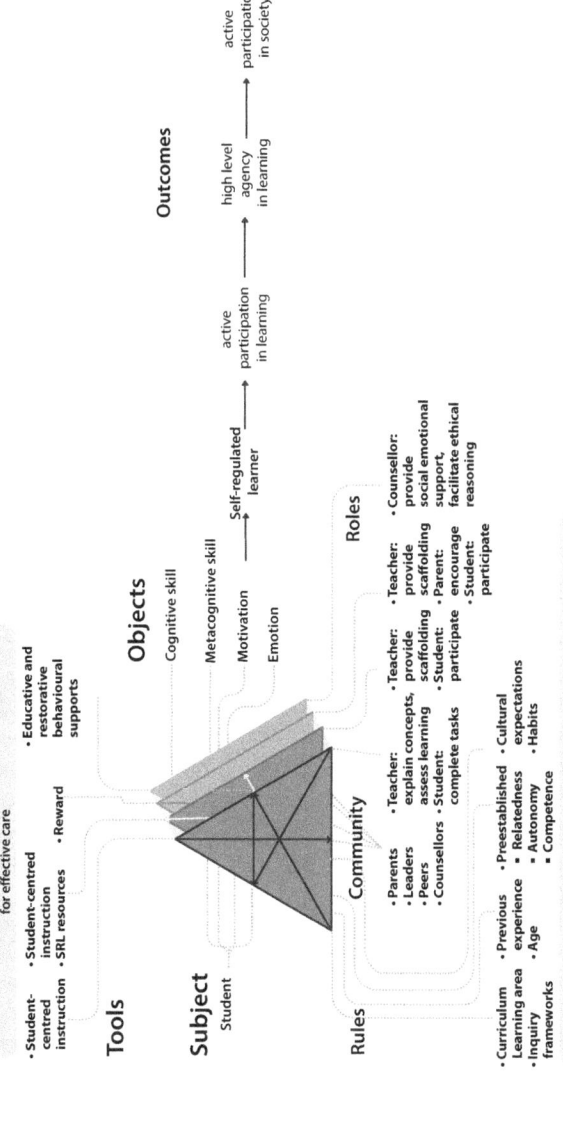

through feedback loops, they can create tensions and/or enablers that influence the outcome of the activity(s).

There are two main types of feedback loops: balancing and reinforcing. A balancing feedback loop occurs when one element increases a behaviour, and the other decreases it. A simple example is a thermostat; one element in the thermostat senses a cold temperature and turns a heater on. When the environment gets too hot, a second element senses this warmth and turns the heater off. They can go around in the loop indefinitely, keeping the room temperature in relative equilibrium.

The second type of feedback loop is a reinforcing feedback loop, where the two elements amplify each other's behaviour. Two dogs, Toto and Lassie, meet for the first time. Toto gets excited about Lassie and chases her. Lassie, getting excited about Toto's excitement, chases Toto back. Both dogs feed on each other's excitement, eventually getting so overwhelmed that their humans pull them apart.

These feedback loops are simple, and there is nothing inherently good or bad about the behaviours the arise from them, but they can get quite messy as more elements become involved. Balancing feedback loops can cause systemic inertia resulting in a system that is resistant to change, or they can cause systemic resilience, meaning that a system quickly bounces back to its initial state after being prodded. Reinforcing loops, if left unmoderated, can ultimately lead to system instability and overload. An unfortunately relatable reinforcing feedback loop is the endless 'reply all' email chain. Imagine an email has been sent to the whole school, and Kate has accidentally hit 'reply all' when clarifying some information. Raj responds to Kate, but has mistakenly also hit reply all. Morgan, feeling helpful, decides to let Kate and Raj know of their mistaken 'reply all' … by replying all. Lin doesn't realise this is all a mistake and lets everyone know – via reply all – his thoughts on the matter, to which Kate responds, once again, via reply all. Eventually everyone's inboxes are full of nonsense. Even though they have potential to result in chaotic behaviour, reinforcing loops can still be useful, particularly when there is a desire to cause change to the system.

In an activity, these feedback loops can arise in many ways. It may be that Winnie is struggling with a concept, but her friend encourages her to keep trying, encouraging Winnie until she understands. Seeing Winnie's improvement, the friend puts in more effort to help out and Winnie improves even more. This is a reinforcing feedback loop that enables Winnie to thrive in the activity. But on the other hand, Winnie may be feeling anxious about an assessment and perform poorly. Seeing this result, she starts to feel more anxious and, over time, her performance plummets. This feedback between anxiety and obligations to perform well on an assessment could cause a tension that prevents that Winne from thriving. Taking a systems thinking approach, it is quite possible both of these loops are affecting Winnie at once. To illustrate this, let's look at one of Winnie's activities, where the object is conceptual understanding (Figure 5.7).

Identifying tensions begins by looking at which parts of the system might interact with the object or outcome. These often arise at the boundaries between elements, such as between a rule or social norm and the implementation of a tool, or the use of a tool and the anticipated outcome. Often, they will lead to non-linear consequences that can't be seen unless we look at the whole system.

Figure 5.7 shows three clear tensions:

- Tension A: The Australian curriculum highlights learning areas defined by conceptual understanding of content, but high assessment scores may not truly measure understanding.

Neoliberal education is often based on a simple premise: put enough knowledge in a child's head, and they will become an excellent future worker. This has influenced how curricula are written and, more importantly, how they are interpreted by

Figure 5.7: Tensions in a student's activity system that may affect long-term outcomes

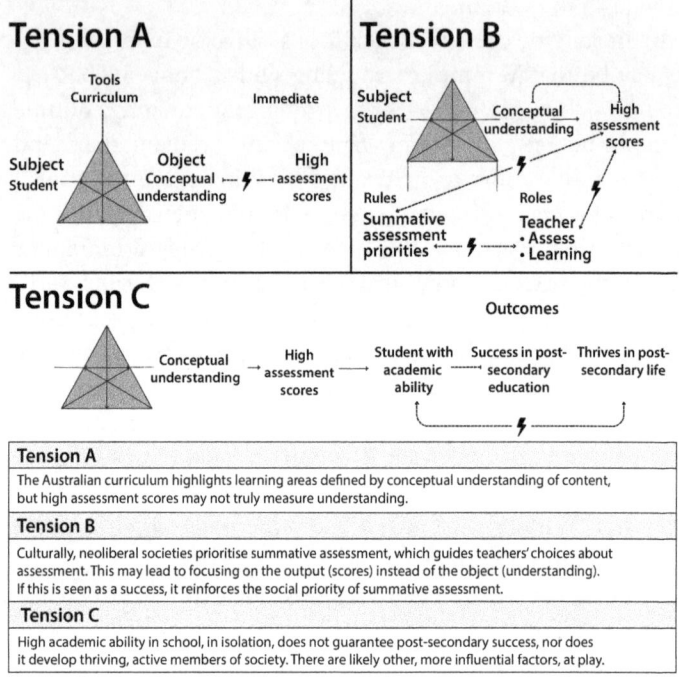

Tension A
The Australian curriculum highlights learning areas defined by conceptual understanding of content, but high assessment scores may not truly measure understanding.
Tension B
Culturally, neoliberal societies prioritise summative assessment, which guides teachers' choices about assessment. This may lead to focusing on the output (scores) instead of the object (understanding). If this is seen as a success, it reinforces the social priority of summative assessment.
Tension C
High academic ability in school, in isolation, does not guarantee post-secondary success, nor does it develop thriving, active members of society. There are likely other, more influential factors, at play.

practitioners. For example, if a curriculum requires a practitioner to develop an understanding of cell organelles *and* to establish strong skills in communication, the first curriculum point is often emphasised above the second, purely because it appears up front and centre in the text. This also means that assessments may be designed to capture Winnie's knowledge of a cell, with little assessment of her ability to communicate with her peers.

So, imagine we are measuring our success by the outcome: a multiple-choice quiz on cell organelles. Immediately, we can see conceptual understanding doesn't necessarily lead to high test scores because other factors might be at play. In our previous example, Winnie experienced test anxiety, which is a norm within her personal system that affects her behaviour. She may be a passionate biology enthusiast who writes songs about cell organelles in her free time, her performance in *tests* may be so heavily influenced by her own anxiety that she ends up with a very low score. On the other hand, it is possible that a student could perform well even without high conceptual understanding if they rote-learned the answers, or even cheated. This relationship causes a tension between the object and outcome, because we may be incorrectly describing conceptual understanding through performance. But this also highlights another relationship in Tension B:

- Tension B: Culturally, neoliberal societies prioritise summative assessment, which guides teachers' choices about assessment. This may lead to focusing on the objects measured by this form of assessment (say, discrete pieces of knowledge) instead of the outcome (say, conceptual understanding). If this is seen as a success, it reinforces the social priority of summative assessment.

Regardless of our intensions to help Winnie thrive in life, leaders are constantly under pressure to meet neoliberal metrics. Because neoliberal philosophies reduce students down to a number, university entrance scores, exams and other forms of summative assessment are socially and culturally prioritised as measures of success.

This means that in the role teachers have in assessing student learning, they are more likely to make choices that provide a nice, neat, easily comparable number, often in a standardised format. They may make choices on what to assess based on the curriculum and *how* to assess it based on this societal priority. If they, personally and professionally, are under pressure to show their impact through these assessment metrics, it may shift the focus of the activity from conceptual understanding (the outcome) to assessment performance (the immediately visible object), unintentionally redefining the objective of the activity.

In this case, we may see a scenario where a school or class produces very highly scoring students and is therefore deemed successful and worthy of better perks or funding. In turn, this may reinforce the social view that summative assessment scores are the more important metric of success, creating a big feedback loop that spans across rules, roles and outcomes. But this societal norm is also based on a neoliberal – and therefore flawed – theory of change.

- Tension C: High academic achievement in school, in isolation, does not guarantee post-secondary success, nor does it develop a thriving, active member of society. There are likely other, more influential factors, at play.

Tension 3 represents a tension between the immediate outcome and the long-term outcome, because of an incorrect assumption that academic ability (or, in the previous example, high test scores) is the biggest factor that leads to success in life. Tensions 1 and 3 are both examples of tensions that arise from assumptions, so it is sometimes easiest to find tensions and enablers based on the assumptions you've identified in your theory of change. We chose to focus on the 'understanding' system precisely because the 'popular' theory of change drives reductionist, neoliberal tendencies, so Winnie's understanding system becomes the point of focus.

In this case, we know that there are myriad other reasons Winnie does or does not become a willingly active member of society. Let's imagine that Winnie's teacher provided explicit instruction on how to write a structured essay by following the format preferred by her final examiners, covering each of the themes of the book they are studying in detail. As a result, Winnie receives excellent marks in her essay about Frankenstein and is excited to enter her first year as a literature student.

However, her dreams of university don't match the reality. First, she finds they she is suddenly given more autonomy over her own learning than she can handle and doesn't have personal strategies for self-regulated learning and loses motivation. Next, all her peers seem like they are excellent students when she alone struggles, and her self-efficacy crumbles, so she finds it hard to make friends and learn socially. Finally, she realises she didn't really understand the themes of Frankenstein at all, she simply rewrote what her teacher had told her, so she feels like she doesn't know how to critically analyse texts to make new connections. All of this results in her leaving university after one semester. Her academic achievement was simply insufficient to overcome the future obstacles and, in some places, the focus on her exam scores may have prevented other activities (for example, metacognitive, motivation, and so on) that could have supported her through the transition.

This may feel like an extreme example, but it's a reality of many university students. Thus, the neoliberal philosophy of academic achievement equates to success in life is simply unfit for our intentions to develop thriving adults.

These examples all show how teachers' pedagogical choices could affect Winnie. While there will be many more enablers and tensions in Winnie's activity system, especially when considering external factors – for example, wellbeing – we can see that we must look beyond her own system to address some of these issues. This is where it becomes apparent that leaders are often needed at levels where rapid adaptation and decision making is needed at the micro level. And where will these leaders come from? The system that is already in place, of course.

Relating teacher professional development with student outcomes

Winnie's success is heavily tied to the support structures that allow her to thrive. We know the community and division of labour around Winnie's activity system can create powerful tensions or enablers. It is therefore pragmatic to look at other activities that support her system, too, because this will reveal horizontal tensions between systems that are invisible in isolation. For example, teachers and school leaders have a high level of responsibility in Winnie's activities, and their presence informs how activity is carried out. We can think of a teacher's activity as an enabling system for Winnie because they provide a support structure to Winnie's learning. But Winnie's teacher is also continuously undergoing complex activity as they grow and develop as a teacher who makes impactful pedagogical choices. As Winnie's teacher develops, this will feed back into Winnie's system (Figure 5.8). So, if better system structures are in place for teachers to perform their role, it would benefit not only Winnie, but all of her classmates. On the other hand, elements in the teacher's activity may also create tensions that affect Winnie, so the two systems must be viewed as inextricably linked.

When we modelled these two systems, it became apparent that teachers were trying to navigate class size and a culture of standardisation that is typical in Australian schools. This compromised their flexibility in pedagogical choices, which made it difficult to balance individual student needs. We cannot only look at Winnie's systems of activity and not react to the horizontal enablers and tensions caused by the teacher system.

Professional certificate

So, we once again get back to the importance of navigating complexity as leaders. However, this is where we saw another major system tension. If it is so complex, whose responsibility is it to unravel and respond to the complexity? It takes a village to navigate complexity, so to speak, so who has the role of reacting to dynamic and adaptive systems? *Who can lead this change in a scalable way?* Some of the community around Winnie must have this role but, at present, it did not appear that this was a defined responsibility in her activity systems (Figure 5.9).

At a glance, we may attribute the responsibility of navigating complexity to leaders in an administrative structure, but inspecting Winnie's day to day activity, it was apparent that

Figure 5.8: Impact of teaching activity on student activity

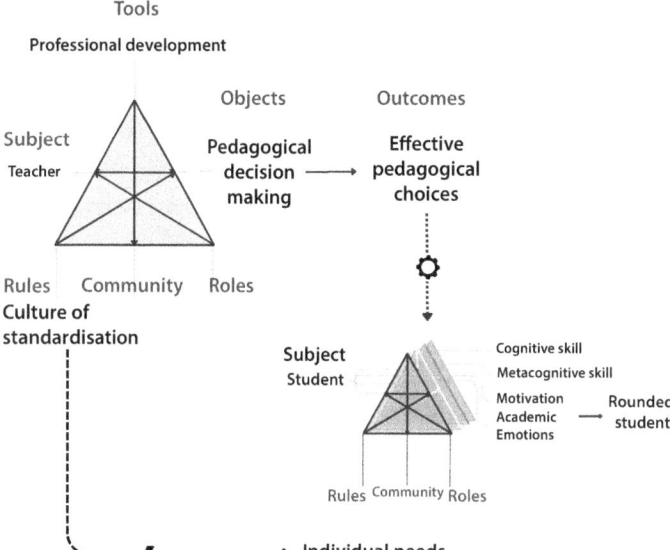

there was a high amount of variability and change within her immediate environment that required leadership in her more immediate activity. In trying to establish this role, however, we also found that there was a skill deficit in complexity thinking that first needed to be addressed. We also realised that there was a rich cohort of future leaders that could become effective complexity thinkers in their own right. Instead of bringing in new complexity thinkers, why don't we develop leaders in the community that already understand the cultural nuances of CFC?

So, we established a group of community members who could apply complexity thinking. In this activity, a group of teachers are the subjects of a professional development activity system, where the object of transformation is their complexity thinking (Figure 5.10).

This activity was already some experiencing major tensions from the beginning of the project; namely, teachers already

Figure 5.9: Modelling across complex systems

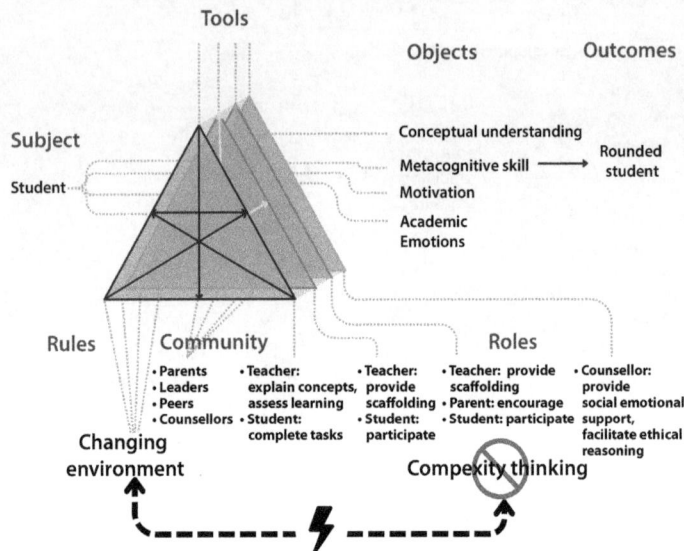

Note: The dashed arrow represents a potential tension. Complexity thinking did not appear as a responsibility of the teacher in any system, despite a changing environment.

carried such a high cognitive load that they may not be motivated or have time to carry out the extra work, especially if it didn't appear to have a tangible outcome (Figure 5.10). A second, but enabling factor, was that professional relationships between staff were built on shared respect, making this a good environment for social learning (Figure 5.10). Together, this tension and enabler led us to develop a *Professional Certificate in Futures Oriented Learning*, where interested teachers could gain a tangible qualification while learning with their peers. To support this, CFC specifically released participants in the professional certificate to manage their cognitive and time load.

The professional certificate was a micro-credentialed version of two of the courses from our Master of Education degree. By taking the micro-credential approach, we did not need to

Figure 5.10: Professional learning activity system

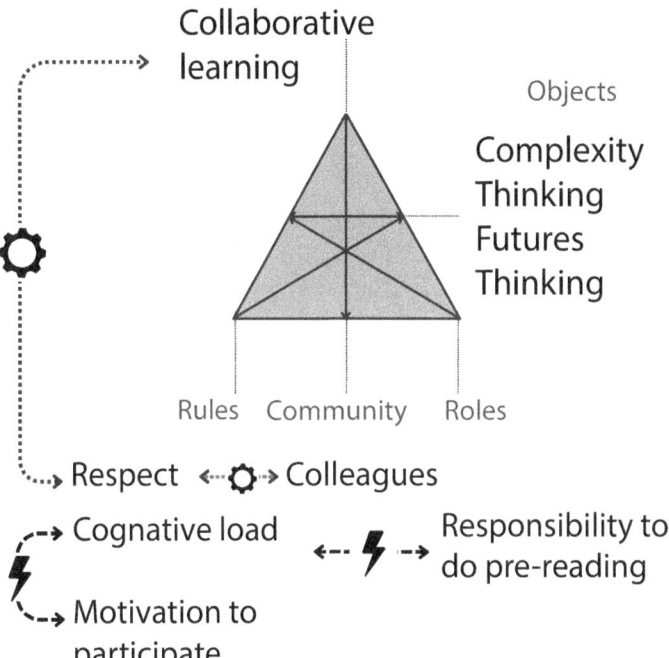

force the collaborative learning into a university timetable. Rather, the participants were able to engage in the learning materials, try out what they'd learned in their own context and at a time that worked for them to do so. They were then able to reconvene to reflect and discuss. The certificate served as a light-touch structure.

Happily, the pilot of the certificate was highly promising, and the first cohort showed a lot of enthusiasm for the process. Many specifically mentioned that the time allowances and the social learning environment were instrumental in their personal learning, and some of the cohort also expressed an interest in developing further or applying their experimentation through a Doctor of Education or Doctor of Philosophy. This was an observable impact of the activity and suggested we had achieved our immediate outcome and were on the way to reaching our intermediate outcome. We were also pleased to see that this was an early indication that new leaders were emerging through the process.

However, in the second interaction of the professional certificate we saw a different outcome. Initially there was enthusiasm about joining the certificate, because teachers had received positive feedback from previous participants, but there were fewer completions in this interaction. One potential reason – among many, we assume – may be that the new cohort had different group dynamics that conflicted with the social learning environment of the certificate. This was a little surprising, but highlighted how important it is to consistently apply PAM and react to new system tensions.

Despite this, the second cohort appeared to greatly benefit from their relationships with the first cohort and still exhibited much of the curiosity the first cohort had demonstrated. This was unexpected, but raised a very interesting question: Was there a flow of information through the informal professional social networks within CFC? Were we seeing the original cohort develop into leaders? Can we use this to leverage more approachable professional development and support for other community members?

Closing the loop by expanding the scope

The unexpected dynamic between the two cohorts prompted us to delve deeper into the patterns and implications of these interactions, setting the stage for a broader investigation into how the leadership of thought leaders and knowledge sharing might evolve within professional communities (Johnson et al, 2024). This project came in response to our anecdotal observations of the informal information sharing that was occurring in CFC, but also in CFC's response to the SAS and WEC data collection. Leadership expressed the desire to make data-informed decisions but were conscious of the gap between what the data said and actionable decision-making. They knew that the data gathered through various collections were valuable, but wanted to ensure that the evolving information and structures were being disseminated right through to CFC.

This provides us with an interesting direction. Could we use Learning Analytics to track how information was being shared following a professional learning activity? Could we use this to see how leadership was emerging within the community? This would clarify if we were on the trajectory to meet the long-term goals stated in the professional certificate activity system.

By analysing social connections between people, we were able to track the decision-making structures across CFC to see how networks of collaboration and influence were shifting. Interestingly, we observed two distinct – but interrelated – structures emerge. One was a formal network of decision making, where decisions were made centrally and disseminated in an outwards direction across formal leaders at CFC. This lacked connectivity, where leadership decisions may have been made in a silo. However, informal networks emerged around individual practitioners following our partnership activities, where they appeared to be spanning the boundaries normally seen within the formal network. Essentially, we were seeing the emergence of new knowledge leaders across different branches of CFC.

However promising this was, we also saw that these informal networks fluctuate in strength and cohesion and could even lead to echo chambers. This new emergent behaviour of this activity system required attention to adapt and ensure the boundary-spanning is actually supported before it falls apart. This meant that unfortunately, though very informative, this sophisticated work isn't accessible to many educators. We adapted to this my making a short video and infographic poster to communicate these findings back to the wider teaching community.

Conclusion

Our relationship with CFC demonstrates how PAM can be a powerful, flexible framework for meaningful change amidst the complexities of an actual, functioning education system. It was clear that traditional models of success – namely, academic success – were insufficient to meet CFC's goal of helping students like Winnie to thrive in their post-secondary lives. But, using PAM to look at the often chaotic, interconnected systems that Winnie and her teachers experienced, we were able to see the 'bigger picture' or enablers and tensions relating to this goal.

The iterative nature of PAM also allowed us to test tangible interventions in 'real time' to ensure they were appropriate for system change. None of the initiatives implemented are static but were continually adapted by practice experts within the systems in a context-specific way, which meant that these adaptable interventions were more likely to be sustainable in the face of unexpected system change.

For those with an eye on theory development, we'd also suggest that the examples outlined in this chapter show that the use of ideas from systems thinking and complexity theory might also offer a way forward with respect to a new generation of Activity Theory (see Spinuzzi and Guile, 2019). Notably, the approach that has emerged in this work, following Uhl-Bien et al (2007), plays far greater attention to the interaction 'between' components of activity systems examined as part of an array of activity or a 'macro-system'.

SIX

Pragmatic Adaptive Leadership: building the supports for self-regulated learning

In this final chapter, we will explore how Pragmatic Adaptive Design (PAD) can be implemented to build upon the understandings that flow from a well-developed practice of Pragmatic Adaptive Modelling (PAM). We will do so by continuing the story of our work with Corroboree Frog College (CFC), although we note that we are now moving into work that is still in progress at the time of writing.

This work in progress we will describe has emerged from our earlier work with CFC. It is evidence of emergent leadership with the college, and, pleasingly, is also increasingly proactive work with respect to the 'thriving after school' problem we started with many years ago. While our earlier work has largely focused on enabling leadership and has used PAM to help key members of the college better understand the dynamic barriers to change, the phase of work we will describe in this chapter leans more heavily into the use of Pragmatic Adaptive *Design* to realise the transformative practices that contribute to the kinds of thriving the school is seeking.

An interesting thing that has emerged – and we choose the word 'emerge' deliberately – from our PAL work with CFC is that a group of educators have elected to use the structure of the PhDs to lead change within their school. Having been deeply involved in our PAM work in previous years, these (emerging) leaders are ideal drivers and enablers of PAL. They have developed a strong understanding of the relevant research literature, and they have a deep and lived experience of the CFC systems. In this chapter, we will discuss how two of these projects being undertaken within the PhD structure are progressing as we consider more closely how PAD can be implemented.

The projects we are discussing in this chapter were relatively new at the time of writing and will adapt and evolve in the years to come, but they both utilise the same frameworks of PAD to make deliberate design choices with observable outcomes. They do so with the ultimate objective of cultivating students' capacity to learn and adapt, challenging the entrenched activity of many schools that focus on the completion of routine tasks and efficient recall (Schwartz, 2024). Instead, they seek to develop and improve the professional understanding of pedagogies and learning environments that foster adaptation and innovation among both students and teachers.

Enabling self-regulated learning

At the outset, these self-regulated learning (SRL) themed projects seem reasonably straightforward. The broad concept of SRL tends to be appealing to most educators. From the inception, however, the project leaders have been all too aware that operationalising SRL is complex and multifaceted. As one of our project leaders reflected:

> I think that staff feel at ease with the idea of SRL because it is essentially underpinned by a holistic view of teaching which, in my opinion, most educators hold themselves. However, asking staff to attend to each of the factors

which shape SRL can bring about extra stress, as we are essentially asking them to individualise their practice even more.

Or, as another of our leaders noted:

> A lack of deep implementation-oriented understanding might be a reason why people get very excited initially about SRL and the idea of explicitly teaching students strategies and skills, but then this excitement gives way to 'overwhelmment' as their to-do lists get too long. Understanding that it is important and believing that it works is not enough to encourage teachers to spend time building understanding, developing different approaches to use with students, teaching students how to choose between a range of strategies. When I think of my emotional reaction as a teacher and a leader working with staff, I feel concern, because I believe that what the majority of staff – committed educators but time poor and overwhelmed – want are quick fixes, specific tasks and activities that they can do with students.

Some of the complexity that teachers are dealing with here is a product of the rapid development of SRL models. Early SRL research largely centred around the cognitive and the individual, but researchers have quickly and increasingly sought to integrate social and affective understandings of learning. To us, with our PAM approach to modelling, this theoretical direction is progressively looking like an array of activity systems within an individual, sitting within a further array of activity systems that are the life of the student – class, school, family and society. And in the still more recent research, there is a growing interest in the concept of shared regulation and the kinds of interactions that foster its development (Hadwin et al, 2017; Järvelä et al, 2023; Singh and Muis, 2024). Within this work, we can identify key objects of transformation.

Against the background of this quite rapid theoretical development, the projects we are discussing here have been quickly driven towards a need to consider exactly the kinds of parallel or simultaneous activity we developed PAM to deal with. One of the projects has been exploring how to manage cognitive load while still supporting motivation, and the other has been mapping the roles and social norms around goal attainment as a step towards designing new approaches to teaching students goal settings. Working in this space, the projects highlight the need for educational leaders to attend to multiple activities when they are seeking to achieve complex outcomes. We have provided a simple model of this change in Figure 6.1, noting that the development of SRL involves activity in (at least) the cognitive, metacognitive, motivational and emotional domains.

However, as the theoretical development around SRL has not yet been translated into *standard* forms of professional practice, there remain numerous questions about how we might undertake this transformation. The tools that work in the 'wilds' of the school have not yet been established, and it is far from clear whose responsibility it is to select and embed new tools. We would also observe that this lack of clarity is one of the major failings of current neoliberal models of educational governance. With their focus on the efficient delivery of the 'known', these systems of governance simply do not deal well with expanding into new forms of practice.

Enabling the macro-system

The Pragmatic Adaptive Leadership (PAL) that is embodied in these projects is emergent from what has gone before. We have started to map this in Figure 6.2. This model is a way of representing how the development of the interrelated systems of SRL within a student is contingent on resolving macro-tensions such as those that might exist between the 'school leadership' activity and the 'teaching' activity. In essence,

PRAGMATIC ADAPTIVE LEADERSHIP

Figure 6.1: Linked systems involved in developing self-regulated learning

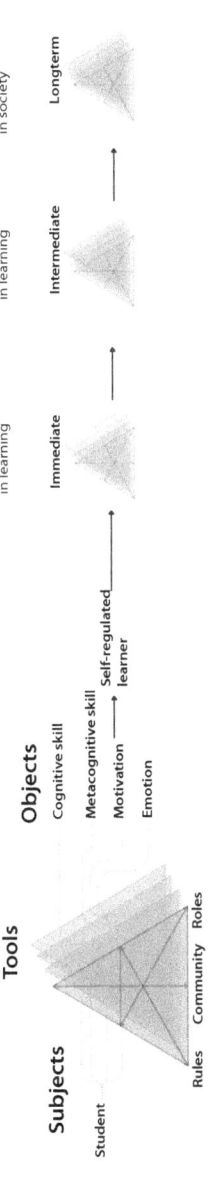

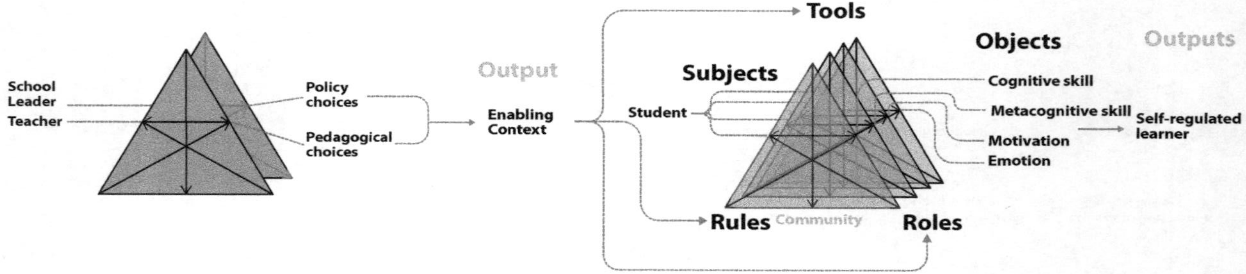

Figure 6.2: Teacher and leader activity supports student activity

this is a way of representing the top-down, bottom-up and enabling forms of leadership we met in Chapter One (Uhl-Bien et al, 2007). It is showing that before we begin to tackle interventions that directly impact SRL, we need to first pay attention to what be thought of as the macro-system that these activities sit within, and to ensure that this macro-system is enabling in nature.

Of course, it is possible to keep zooming out. The teaching and school leadership activity systems each sit within broader structures such as community, discipline and nation. In wider systems and complexity theory, one can zoom out so far that the system of study is the entire universe, although our concern is constrained a little more by its ultimate interest in human learning. When taking the PAL approach, however, decisions of scale are ultimately driven by the scale of our potential influence.

Another thing to recall here is that in Activity Theory, what we might often think of as the 'context' is explicitly a part of the activity system. From an Activity Theory perspective, the activity is mediated by historically and culturally derived rules and tools. That is, the physical, social and cultural environment is very much a part of how we undertake an activity. In the PAL approach, we have been arguing that if we want to shape activity, if we want to *lead* it, then attention must be paid to the interconnected arrays of activities that work towards common objectives. This in turn creates a need to attend to the interconnected 'contexts' of those activities. But as the context is a part of the activity that is occurring, we refer to it as the macro-system.

All of this is a long way of saying that even though the projects we are discussing here build upon the work that has gone before at CFC, they have still necessitated a renewed implementation of the PAM practices. We would argue that effective design is simply not possible without at least some engagement in effective modelling. The first step in these projects, therefore, has been for these leaders to work with their colleagues to develop a shared image of what they thought SRL could look like in their school.

As we saw in the earlier quotes, it has been clear from the beginning that our CFC leaders were now very aware of not falling into the common pitfall of taking a 'tips and tricks' approach to imagining the changes they are seeking. The tips and tricks approach to SRL is deceptively straightforward: incorporating formative feedback on the learning process towards goal attainment, involving students in defining criteria for success, identifying effective strategies and so on. These are small yet meaningful adjustments that can be practically applied within current systems, but rarely are in a sustained fashion. These pedagogies aren't inherently flawed and are even often recommended by experts, but without a deeper understanding of SRL's complexities and the contextual variations of classroom implementation, these practices have limited impact. The schools we work with need to understand not only metacognitive processes, such as those proposed by Zimmerman, or Boekaerts' insights into motivation, but also to synthesise this knowledge into a holistic, school-wide approach to fostering adaptive, strategic learning processes. The PAM model that has developed from this renewed effort is shown in Figure 6.3.

As we can see in Figure 6.3, the model for action that has developed goes well beyond a focus on tips and tricks from the research. Through this modelling, we can see that implementing self-regulated learning activities is a highly complex task, but also that it is possible to break them down to see the individual tensions that occur between activities. Three major tensions have been identified:

- Tension A: A student with pre-existing stress or anxiety often deprioritises certain tasks to alleviate their stress, decreasing their motivation to participate.
- Tension B: Culturally, a school site may restrict experimentation. When the student is given explicit

Figure 6.3: Intersystem tensions in SRL activities

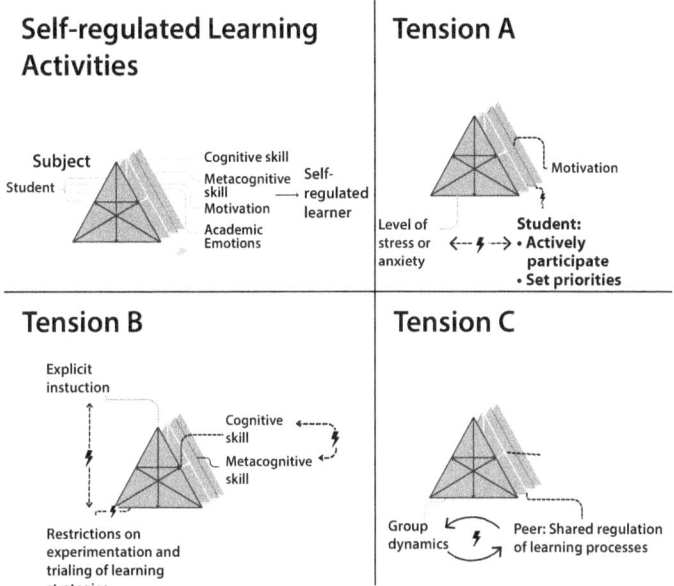

Tension A
A student with pre-existing stress or anxiety may deprioritise certain task to alleviate their stress, decreasing their motivation to participate.
Tension B
Culturally, a school site may rescrrict experimentation. When the student is given only explicitminstuction in this system, they may be unable to trial metacognitive skills that aid cognitive skill.
Tension C
Group dynamics of a class directly affect shared regulation of learning, but this shared learning can feed back into group dnamics. This could perpetuate beneficial OR harmful dynamics that affect the development of metacognitive learning in a social space.

instruction in this system, they may be unable to trial metacognitive skills that aid cognitive skill.
- Tension C: Group dynamics of a class directly affect shared regulation of learning, but this shared learning can feed back into group dynamics. This could perpetuate beneficial *or* harmful dynamics that affect the development of metacognitive learning in a social space.

This exploration of parallel arrays of activity has underpinned the movement of these projects into their PAD or design phase. They have provided a way to identify how we might most productively disrupt elements of the macro-system of schooling that have historically constricted teaching and learning focused on agency.

Pragmatic Adaptive Design: using Pragmatic Adaptive Modelling to make effective design choices

Educational design is a process of planning, creating and refining learning experiences, instructional systems and educational environments. This is all towards a purpose defined by a school site, but all effective design is improved by a systematic approach to ensuring these goals are fulfilled.

In the field, PAD utilised three practices:

- Design Thinking: A life-centred, iterative approach to solving problems, where choices require empathy, creativity and a deep understanding of the end-users' activity systems.
- Research-Informed Design: As the companion of Design-based Research (Anderson and Shattuck, 2012), this is an approach to making design choices based on empirical evidence, theoretical insights, and consideration of real-world applications, where iterations are fed back into the research cycle.
- Reflexive practice: An ongoing process of critically examining actions, choices and assumptions to continuously improve. This is instrumental in recognising how to adapt new tools to meet a system's needs.

The success of PAD is amplified by a diverse range of skills and expertise so adapting research theory with the practical realities of a specific school site like CFC requires researchers to work directly with practitioners in collaboration (Svihla, 2010). Where we, as researchers and leaders, might conduct

PAM and make informed decisions based on the modelling, PAD is most effective in the hands of practitioners, who are experts in the day-to-day business of the school.

Research-Informed Design: making design choices

Research-Informed Design allows us to make deliberate design choices that consider the whole context of an activity. This template (Figure 6.4) provides a guide to ensure that all design is undertaken with an understanding of PAM and research.

Step 1: Literature review

The first step of Research-Informed Design is to understand the theoretical background of the activity. This chapter has demonstrated some of the complexities of SRL, but it has also notably highlighted that there are myriad factors involved in developing a self-regulated learner. This is valuable information that can be drawn upon when developing design standards.

Step 2: Explore the activity systems

The next step is to explore the activity system model that results from PAM, in order to identify some key tensions that need to be at the forefront of our thinking. For example, based on the tensions we identified previously, we may choose to highlight the social learning nature of SRL, and how that affects metacognitive skill and motivation.

Step 3: Review Futures Thinking

All design choices must link back to the goals and objects of transformation determined during Futures Thinking. If the long-term goal is to see students thrive, and we see that SRL is a way towards developing life-long learners who can thrive,

Figure 6.4: Research-Informed Design template

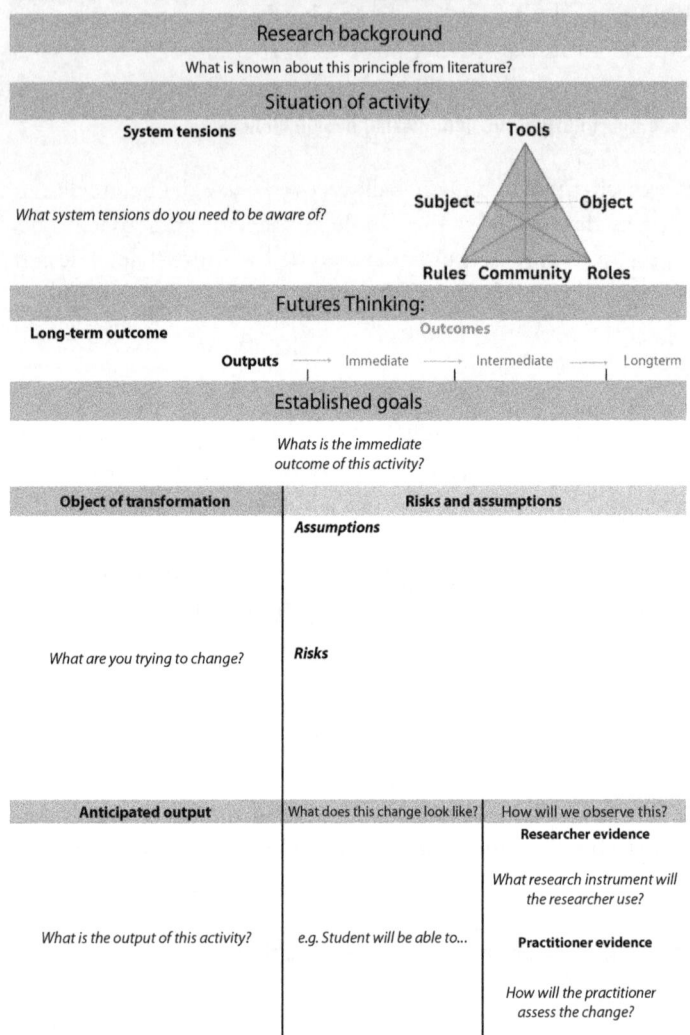

it is evident that students are an evolving system. The first three steps of the design process draw from PAM, but they are necessary to review in the design process because they help to orient ourselves in the big picture, mitigating the risk of falling back on 'simple' but ineffective methods.

Step 4: Review the goal of the activity

This step not only reflects upon the intended immediate outcome of the activity but allows us to evaluate whether the immediate outcome is a true step towards the long-term outcome. It also provides an opportunity to consider what emergent behaviours we hope to see from a successful activity.

From this outcome, we can then establish the object of transformation in the activity and consider exactly what we hope to change. The difference between an object and an outcome is crucial to determine at this step, because it is common to focus on the outcome without much thought of what is actually changing in the student to achieve that outcome. As a general rule of thumb, an object is a noun, and an outcome describes a system behaviour.

Our modelling showed that there are multiple activities that contribute to SRL, all with their own object of transformation, despite sharing a single outcome. If we focus only on the outcome without seeing the different objects, we run the risk of reducing the complex activities involved in SRL to focus only on the 'easiest' object to transform, the object that has the most historical precedence, or unintentionally targeting no object at all. This identification also helps to break down the system into manageable components, to see a small problem in context. This helps scaffold the small, pragmatic decisions that lead to long-term change, instead of trying to manage the huge nebulous problem without direction.

So, having identified our objects, we could design four individual interacting interventions that target cognitive and metacognitive skill, motivation and academic emotions.

Step 5: Identify risks and assumptions

Now we can identify the assumptions in our theory of change. To scaffold this, ask yourself the following questions:

- What needs to happen for this activity to succeed?
- What am I taking for granted that might affect the success of this activity?
- What does 'everything going right' look like, and what could make that happen?

Now, identify the risks that the outcome won't be achieved. Some questions to scaffold this are:

- What could prevent the outcome from happening?
- What if one of the assumptions isn't true?
- What does a worst-case scenario look like, and what could cause that?
- What tensions between systems could prevent the outcome?

This step is particularly powerful in the hands of practitioners, as they are experts in navigating the everyday chaos of the education system. They bring a wealth of knowledge about 'what could realistically happen' and experience on how they have navigated these complexities in real time.

Step 6: Consider how to evaluate the effects of the change

It is important to evaluate whether the design is achieving the desired outcome(s), or we risk designing ineffective interventions. A common pitfall here is to assume that a change in one object of an activity is tantamount to achieving the desired outcome. For example, we tend to assume that the demonstration of constituent knowledge is a strong indicator of conceptual understanding, and so assessment tools such as multiple-choice tests are frequently deployed to evaluate educational activity systems. However, as we know that it's possible that a student's test anxiety may hide their knowledge acquisition or, conversely, that their ability to 'game' the test may give us unwarranted confidence in their knowledge acquisition, it is unlikely that simple forms of assessment will be sufficient to evaluate complex educational activity. Traditional forms of professional judgement may be useful in addressing the evaluation gap here. For example, an educator may decide that a student's ability to 'ask extension questions' is a more accurate indicator of a change in conceptual understanding. The principle to this PAL practice, though, is to actively consider what can and should count as evidence.

The diverse forms of evidence that are possible here also points to the value of researchers and practitioners evaluating educational design together. Researchers acting without practitioners run the risk of generating evaluations that aren't conducive of practical iteration or don't meet stakeholder needs. Practitioners acting without researchers run the risk of identifying and evaluating inappropriate objects of transformation under the pressure of neoliberal standards. Together, however, they are able to identify the utility of different kinds of evidence.

Some forms of evaluation may be:

- learning analytics such as the Student Attitudes Survey;
- self-report assessments of metacognitive strategies;
- semi-structured interviews;
- portfolios.

Step 7: Design Thinking

Design Thinking is a design process that centres on empathising with the end user, and so often melds naturally with educators' ideals. A practitioner can place themselves in the students' shoes to empathise with how the system around them is affecting their learning and imagining solutions that directly play into this context. This step of Design Thinking is particularly important to generate student-centred solutions because it is common to skip to solutions that don't fully target the nuance of a child's complex life. This 'diagnostic' phase is supported by the PAM that lays out the tensions and enablers embedded in the current system.

With this empathy, educational designers can then brainstorm as many ideas as possible towards that problem and generate a divergent range of possibilities. These ideas can then be distilled convergently down to one or two practical and promising ideas for prototyping. These solutions can then be designed and prototyped iteratively, allowing the practitioner flexibility to alter or abandon ideas in response to the system.

Step 8: Explore how the design affects systems

PAD focuses on how the designs can be adapted to meet system needs, but we also know that many complex skills, like SRL, are affected by multiple systems. Figure 6.5 shows a process for evaluating whether the design – be it a protocol, a strategy, an assessment, and so on – is truly informed by research, and whether it conflicts with other systems that could create negative feedback. This example shows three systems, but the same process could be utilised for as many systems as are necessary.

Step 9: Evaluate the design

After the design phase, teachers actively monitor the impact of change with the help of our team. Using 'light touch' instruments that show change over time, such as the School Attitudes Survey, and teacher-instigated measurement methods, such as focus group discussions, we begin to explore whether our theory of change is resulting in the outcomes we are seeking. This information is fed back to school where we further adjust and perfect practices through multiple iterations.

Evaluation takes two forms: research data and practitioner data. These observations can extend beyond numerical evaluation

Figure 6.5: Design evaluation protocol

Design Element			
(Protocol/Activity/Strategy)			
How does this element meet design standards?			
How is this element informed by research?			
	System A	System B	System C
What is the object of transformation?			
How will this design affect the object?			
What research informs this element?			
How does this element affect the system?			
How could is affect intersystem interactions with:			
System A			
System B			
System C			

and include qualitative and observational information about the behaviours and norms arising in the classroom. The researcher data is important to highlight hidden and nuanced trends that may occur across time, which informs PAM. The practitioner data is important for ensuring changes are translated to the needs of the school site and capitalises on the expertise of practitioners to leverage evaluation methods that may be absent from research (for example, observations about the immediate classroom climate to respond to individual needs).

Evaluation is an ongoing process that feeds back into the iteration of design choices. It is important to continuously monitor and evaluate designs because the system will change as new behaviours emerge, which may make it less receptive to the interventions.

This can be illustrated easily by thinking of a class's dynamics, which deeply affect students' social learning and choices for metacognitive process. Each student will have their own academic and non-academic goals, which are influenced by their families, friends and personalities. In a class that is highly autonomous and friendly towards each other, they may be well positioned to experiment with metacognitive process and support each other in learning, but they may also become distracted by each other and lose motivation to engage in cognitive learning. Will the next class have the same behaviours and dynamics? Will they require the exact same supports as the previous class, or will interventions need adapting to meet the new students' attitudes?

Just like a class is different every year, so is an activity system, so monitoring these changes over time and using the information to inform interactions is crucial for effective long-term change.

Step 10: Reflexive Review

One of the key practices of PAL is the development of epistemic fluency in the organisation going through the process. Epistemic fluency describes the ability to understand, coordinate and work across different forms of knowledge and ways of knowing (Goodyear and Markauskaite, 2018). We ask our partners to shift between system goals and metrics, the empirical knowledge illustrating potential solutions and problems and the teachers' practical experience of the classroom through the process of forming the modelling. This epistemic fluency is key to considering 'wicked problems' as it allows for more adaptable responses to the dynamic changes that are inherent in any shift in habitus.

Reflexivity – the ability to critically examine one's own beliefs, values and experiences to inform future practices – supports the development of epistemic fluency. A key benefit of reflexivity is the creation of *grounded, actionable knowledge* which is the shared understanding essential for forward-thinking actions linked to findings and practice. However, this actionable knowledge remains specific to the cycle it represents, evolving as new activities are incorporated into future iterations.

Reflexive Review involves critical consideration of the system, the intervention, and how our own values and biases may affect the effectiveness of the design. At an individual level, this can be done by reflection on the process with open-ended questions about the design. Some questions to scaffold this are:

- What parts of the design were effective, and what would you change?
- How did the object of transformation change, and how do you know this?
- How effective was the design in meeting the outcomes?
- How did you adapt the design to different contexts?
- How do my personal goals align to the organisational goals, and the implementation of this design?
- Are there recurring patterns of tension or contradiction in my work? How can I overcome them?
- What am I most proud of in this work, and what do I want to improve?

- What system changes did I observe, and what behaviours might emerge?

Reflexive practice is also effective in pairs or in a group with trusted colleagues, as it can provide new perspectives and ideas that may be difficult to identify in isolation.

Iteration: a marathon, not a sprint

The whole practice of Design-Based Research is contingent on iteration and responding to change, which means it may take months or years to see desired emergent behaviours. What makes this such a powerful tool in the hands of practitioners is that one practitioner with high Research-Informed Design skill can impact the lives of thousands of students. This means that PAD is not just a useful methodology, but a highly valued mindset with wide-reaching consequences.

Conclusion

The governance systems we have around schools at present tend to seek a simple and certain answer to what is best in education, no matter the futility. Many in the teaching profession and in educational research will lament the low value our society currently places on philosophy and introspection. Nevertheless, our society favours the measurable, even when that means we end up measuring things that are just not that important. In this book we have offered some tools that respond to the limitations of the current obsession with simple metrics and proffer instead a pathway towards taking professional stewardship (French et al, 2023) of the diverse and complex outcomes of schooling that our young people and our society actually need.

The approach this book has outlined has been based in modelling. In short, this book has argued that the most effective way to take action within complex systems, with their non-linear effects, feedback loops and emergent properties, is to develop clear models of how we think the system is working and how we think we can design effective and sustainable change. It is in the building of these models that we find the things that are actually worth measuring. In our own work we have found, for example, that student 'attitude' may actually be more important with respect to long-term engagement than student achievement, and so we have turned our attention to measuring the more salient factor.

Clearly more work from both researchers and professionals in needed in order to identify the most meaningful metrics for education as it occurs in different contexts. Further research is also needed on how leaders can make best use of the kinds of models and metrics we promote (Johnson et al, 2024). Our pragmatic approach towards leadership captures the complexities of modern education well. However, it also requires the educational leader to become comfortable with uncertainty. PAM describes the mechanisms and processes of learning, but it does not specify how to measure effective learning or mandate a particular approach to the evaluation of learning activities. Rest assured, this is a deliberate decision. While it is natural for leaders to want to know the efficacy of their actions, the metrics needed to capture the vast array of learning can sometimes be as complex and varied as the learning system itself, so the discussion could fill a whole book itself.

Nevertheless, it is important to highlight the power of PAM in identifying *what* to measure, for *whom*, and *when*, as this paves the way for identifying meaningful metrics of success. For example, in the SRL scenario shown in Figure 6.3, the objects of transformation are cognitive and metacognitive skills, so the instrument needs to measure *changes* in these specific objects. To evaluate this, it is important to select measures that are appropriate for the subject's (that is, a student's) age, developmental stage and any other influencing factors. From a linear perspective, we might adopt a simple measurement instrument, but our PAM reveals that this may unintentionally misrepresent the actual drivers of change – in this case, it would look like the intervention doesn't work, when it is actually the social norms of explicit teaching (Tension B) that are preventing transformation of the object. Therefore, the activity must be designed to explicitly remove or 'switch off' the conflicting social norms during the activity for any changes to be accurately captured. This example demonstrates that evaluation is much more than choosing a good instrument. It really requires an examination of the whole activity system to be sure the instrument is validly capturing *meaningful* data.

It is evident that influencing factors can be easily overlooked, but, thanks to the revealing power of PAM, a pragmatic leader can make informed decisions about measuring change and be confident about the outcome of any evaluation.

Diversity, equity and inclusion

In this book we have argued that education is always complex. In our city, however, the phrase 'complex school site' is commonly used to describe schools that serve groups of students that have traditionally not been well served by our education system. We have found PAM to be particularly useful when we are working in the context of diversity, equity and inclusion (DEI). DEI is actually not the form of words we use for equity work in our country. As we write, however, so much of the work of our friends and colleagues in the United States is under grievous attack, so we use this formulation in solidarity.

Even in the absence of direct political attack, improving the equity of educational systems has proven to be extraordinarily difficult in virtually all parts of the world. A contributing factor, we would argue, has been the lack of professional tools to fully account for the complex and interacting causes of educational disadvantage. The practices of PAM, we would argue further, begin to address this professional need by providing ways to represent the mechanisms that exclude different groups of students in ways that make sense within the day-to-day context of teachers' work.

One example of our own work in this area concerns equity and inclusion for women in Science, Technology, Engineering and Mathematics (STEM; Devis et al, 2023). We know that diversity in STEM is necessary for solving wicked real-world problems because it allows for new perspectives and innovations that are difficult to achieve in homogeneous groups. However, despite decades of interventions, retention of women in STEM remains low in Australia, especially in leadership positions.

The typical STEM outreach programme for schoolgirls involves *inspiring* them to pursue STEM careers, but it is clear this this has not been effective in closing the gender gap in many STEM industries. Noting this, we re-examined our own STEM outreach programmes using PAM to see if there were new ways we could approach the issue and found two impactful insights. First, we found that girls reported that they did not feel they could be *creative* in STEM but displayed higher intentions to pursue STEM subjects when they were applying their creativity to solve STEM-related problems (Vieira et al, 2024). Second, we found that girls who had strong communities of *peers* – not just mentors – demonstrated higher involvement in STEM programmes and subjects.

Using these findings, we reoriented our STEM equity programmes to specifically target creative confidence as an object of transformation by creating a programme where girls were explicitly taught Design Thinking frameworks. The programme was bolstered through a design principle of social learning, where girls connected with and solved problems with girls from other schools, in order to develop and grow their own networks of support. These changes have shown great promise, as girls report that they are now able to see themselves as creative problem solvers, and of seeing STEM as a framework in which they can create meaningful change.

Our work here is nascent, but we have seen how PAL can challenge ingrained programme assumptions, and how it can lead to taking concrete action. The potential for research–practice partnerships here is encouraging.

Theory

We hope that readers might note the contribution this book has made in theory development as well as in school leadership. Engeström's theory of expansive learning and development of a third generation of Activity Theory was powerful in adding the concept of the 'Division of Labour' to earlier work exploring cultural-historical activity. It allowed us to analyse activity that involved more than one actor, albeit while retaining a focus on a particular subject. The approach we have outlined here with our Theory of PAL adds a further nuance by drawing upon concepts from complexity theory.

PAL recognises that, in pursuing complex goal-oriented objectives such as the public policy outcomes sought through formal education, we frequently need to engage in the transformation not of single objects, but of many. To account for this, our approach has been to move away from the standard practice of Activity System Analysis which tends to consider how one activity cascades into another, and instead to examine how activity systems occur in parallel. In doing so, we have also highlighted the utility for both leaders and researchers to attend closely to the interactions and tensions not only within an activity, but *between* arrays of activity. In short, to attend to the macro-systems within which individual activity is nested. In making this case, we are not suggesting that we should move away from activity as a highly useful unit of analysis. Indeed, for the purpose of intervention and leading desired change in school, we would argue that the consideration of arrays of activity leads to far more concrete – and therefore actionable – models than those that emerge from more nebulous concepts of practice.

What are we leading?

We began this book by suggesting that it would be about leadership in the midst of complexity, and that it might provide some tools for the enactment of the wider educational research evidence within the everyday practices of schools. We were even brave enough to suggest that the tools we've been outlining here might be useful in the face of the deficiencies of neoliberal governance and the policy direction our field has experienced under its influence in recent decades. We have tried to do all of this in a short format book and will now try to do it again in a final paragraph.

If our readers take away just one thing from this book, we would like it to be this. Leadership in schools requires an understanding that in schools, and in a student's learning and development, there is always more than one thing going on. Learning, for example, is a practice that involves the cognitive, social, emotional, cultural and many other domains besides. Schools are always under top-down, bottom-up and horizontal pressures to achieve myriad outcomes both for their students and our societies. Leadership, therefore, can never be about simply finding the 'right' solution. Seeking the right solution in the complex set of interconnected systems makes no more sense than seeking the 'best' way for an animal to survive on Earth. If we look at the diversity of plants, animals and fungi around us, we can see that the solutions to the complex 'life on earth' problem are countless. When understood through the lens of complexity, the same is true for the 'way to do school' problem.

Glossary

21st-century skills   A set of abilities that have been identified by the Partnership for 21st Century Learning (Trilling and Fadel, 2009) as being essential to success in a rapidly changing, interconnected world. They include the 4Cs of Communication, Collaboration, Creativity and Critical Thinking.

3GAT (third generation Activity Theory)   A framework developed by Engeström that aims to understand human activities within organisations and emphasises the participatory nature of activity.

4GAT (fourth generation Activity Theory)   A proposed extension to 3GAT that considers the web of participatory practices by incorporating multiple perspectives, transient collaboration, and the interactions across parallel activity systems.

Activity Theory (AT)   A framework for understanding human activity and their contexts, rooted in the work of Vygotsky, Luria, Leontiev and Engeström.

Adaptive leadership   A 'bottom-up' creative and emergent activity which drives change.

GLOSSARY

Administrative leadership — 'Top-down' leadership traditional to schools where a principal makes most of the decisions, sometimes with the assistance of other heads of school.

Capital (Bourdieu) — Resources and assets used to gain social advantage and establish a position within a specific field.

Cognitive Load Theory — An instructional theory centred on the limitations of working memory and strategies for optimising learning.

Community (Activity Theory Concept) — The people that affect the object, directly or indirectly.

Communities of Practice (CoP) — Groups of people who engage in collective learning through ongoing interaction and collaboration.

Complexity Leadership Theory — A theory exploring the dynamic process emerging from the interaction of individuals and systems within complex, adaptive environments.

Corroboree Frog College (CFC) — The school we have commonly worked with in the past.

Cultural-Historical Activity Theory (CHAT) — See Activity Theory

Design-Based Research (DBR) — An interventionist research methodology that develops theory and practical implementation through iterative cycles of practitioner-supported mixed methods investigation within authentic contexts.

Design Thinking — A human-centred problem-solving approach that emphasises creativity, empathy, and iterative thinking to develop innovative solutions to complex challenges.

Enabling leadership — A form of leadership that focuses on creating the conditions for adaptability, collaboration, and innovation in complex systems by acting as a bridge between administrative and adaptive leadership.

Epistemic fluency — The ability to understand, co-ordinate and work across different forms of knowledge and ways of knowing.

Expansive Learning Theory — A social learning theory developed by Engeström and building on the work of Vygotsky and Leontov.

Field (Bourdieu) — Social space or domain of activity where people compete for resources, recognition and power.

Futures Modelling (PAM) — A method by which we identify visible and testable conjectures but without reducing our complex systems to a simple, linear equation.

Futures Thinking (PAM) — A strategic approach to critically considering future scenarios in order to define a preferred path forward.

GLOSSARY

Generative Artificial Intelligence — A technology that uses machine learning techniques to analyse patterns in data and generate outputs like text, images, music and code.

Habitus (Bourdieu) — Deeply ingrained habits and ways of thinking that are developed through experience.

Illusio (Bourdieu) — An investment in the value and significance of a particular field, often reinforcing an individual's continued engagement within that field.

Metacognition — The awareness and regulation of your own thinking processes.

Neoliberalism — A political and economic ideology centred on free markets, individual responsibility and measurable outcomes, often manifesting in education as the commodification of knowledge and the treatment of students as consumers.

New Public Governance (NPG) — A governance model that leverages modern technology to expand participation in policy development and implementation.

New Public Management (NPM) — A framework for reform based on the implementation of neoliberal principles.

Neo-Weberian State (NWS) — A model of governance that blends traditional, rule-based bureaucracy with modern approaches to make governments more responsive, efficient and citizen-focused.

Object of transformation (Activity Theory concept)	What is being changed.
Objective (Activity Theory concept)	What is generated by the activity. We tend to refer to this as an 'Outcome' in PAL.
OECD transformative competencies	A set of skills and abilities necessary for future citizens. They are creating new value, reconciling tensions and dilemmas and taking responsibility.
Outcome (Activity Theory concept)	What is generated by the activity. This is often referred to as the 'Objective' in CHAT.
Parallel activity	The process in Pragmatic Adaptive Modelling of formally modelling two or more activity systems.
Practice architectures	The contextual affordance and constraints which shape our sayings, doings and relatings.
Pragmatic Adaptive Design (PAD)	A structured approach to making change in complex educational systems.
Pragmatic Adaptive Leadership (PAL)	A theory of research translation that aims at addressing the wicked problems of education.
Pragmatic Adaptive Modelling (PAM)	A dynamic, iterative approach to solving real-world problems, especially in complex systems like schools.
Practice theories	A group of social theories focused on repeated, patterned actions or activities.

Randomised control trial (RCT)	A quantitative research method used to test the effectiveness of an intervention by randomly assigning participants to either an experimental group or a control group.
Reflexive Review (PAD)	Reflecting on the impacts of design changes using empirical evidence to identify improvements, while accounting for the complexity of model building, design processes in other PAL practices, and the diverse entanglement of lived activity.
Research-Informed Design (PAD)	The creation of learning designs based on the findings of contemporary research.
Roles (Activity Theory concept)	How task and responsibilities are shared among the people in the system.
Rules (Activity Theory concept)	Guidelines and social norms that affect behaviour.
School Attitudes Survey (SAS)	An instrument to measure students' attitudes towards their learning areas (Kennedy et al, 2016).
Science of Learning and Development (SoLD)	A model of effective school and classroom practices derived by (Darling-Hammond et al, 2020) from the fields of neuroscience, psychology, sociology, developmental and learning sciences.
Simultaneous activity	In Activity Theory, we are interested in the systems of activity that transform an object with a specific objective or purpose. In schools there are many activities occurring at the same time.

Situation Mapping (PAM)	An exploration of a school's current practices using activity theory mapping, including an analysis of the tensions within the system.
Self-regulated learning (SRL)	The 'ways that learners systematically activate and sustain their cognitions, motivations, behaviours, and affects, toward the attainment of their goals' (Schunk and Greene, 2017, p 1).
Subjects (Activity Theory concept)	The primary actor in the activity.
System	A collection of interrelated and/or interacting elements that function together towards a specific purpose or goal.
Systems thinking	A way of viewing complex problems as an interconnected whole instead of as individual parts or elements.
Theory of Change (ToC)	A hypothesis that outlines how and why a specific intervention is expected to achieve its desired outcomes.
Tools (Activity Theory concept)	Resources and instruments to achieve an outcome.
Wellbeing and Engagement Collection (WEC) survey	A measure of a range of non-academic factors that might affect learning commonly used in South Australia.
Wicked problem	A problem that is difficult to define and even more difficult to solve.

References

ACARA (nd) *Foundation to Year 10 Curriculum*. Available at: https://www.australiancurriculum.edu.au/

Anagnostopoulos, D., Lingard, B. and Sellar, S. (2016) Argumentation in educational policy disputes: Competing visions of quality and equity. *Theory into Practice*, 55(4), 342–351. https://doi.org/10.1080/00405841.2016.1208071

Anderson, T. and Shattuck, J. (2012) Design-based research: A decade of progress in education research? *Educational Researcher*, 41(1), 16–25. https://doi.org/10.3102/0013189x11428813

Ball, I., Banerjee, M., Holliman, A. and Tyndall, I. (2024) Investigating success in the transition to university: A systematic review of personal risk and protective factors influencing academic achievement. *Educational Psychology Review*, 36(2), Article 52. https://doi.org/10.1007/s10648-024-09891-0

Bandura, A. (1986) *Social Foundations of Thought and Action*. Prentice Hall.

Barbana, S., Dumay, X. and Dupriez, V. (2020) Accountability policy forms in European education systems: An introduction. *European Educational Research Journal*, 19(2), 87–93. https://doi.org/10.1177/1474904120907252

Barbrook-Johnson, P. and Penn, A.S. (2022) Theory of change diagrams. In P. Barbrook-Johnson and A.S. Penn (eds) *Systems Mapping: How to Build and Use Causal Models of Systems* (pp 33–46). Springer International Publishing. https://doi.org/10.1007/978-3-031-01919-7_3

Barzelay, M. (2001) *The New Public Management: Improving Research and Policy Dialogue* (1st edn). University of California Press. https://doi.org/10.1525/9780520925274

Beckman, B. (2001) Civil society and alliance politics. In B. Beckman, E. Hansson, and A. Sjögren (eds) *Civilis Society and Authoritatianism in the Third World: A Conference Book* (pp 49–68). Department of Polictical Science of Stokholm University.

Beer, S. (1984) The viable system model: Its provenance, development, methodology and pathology. *Journal of the Operational Research Society*, 35(1), 7–25. https://doi.org/10.1057/jors.1984.2

Biesta, G. (2010) *Good Education in an Age of Measurement: Ethics, Politics, Democracy* (Vol 33). Taylor & Francis. https://doi.org/10.4324/9781315634319

Biesta, G. (2015) On the two cultures of educational research, and how we might move ahead: Reconsidering the ontology, axiology and praxeology of education. *European Educational Research Journal*, 14(1), 11–22. https://doi.org/10.1177/1474904114565162

Boekaerts, M. (2011) Emotions, emotion regulation, and self-regulation of learning. In B.J. Zimmerman and D.H. Schunk (eds) *Handbook of Self-regulation of Learning and Performance* (pp 408–425). Routledge.

Boisot, M. and McKelvey, B. (2011) Complexity and organization–environment relations: Revisiting Ashby's law of requisite variety. In P. Allen, S. Maguire and B. McKelvey (eds) *The SAGE Handbook of Complexity and Management* (pp 279–298). SAGE. https://doi.org/10.4135/9781446201084.n16

Bourdieu, P. (1977) *Outline of a Theory of Practice*. Cambridge University Press.

Bourdieu, P. (1996) *The Rules of Art: Genesis and Structure of the Literary Field*. Stanford University Press.

Bourdieu, P. and Wacquant, L.J.D. (1992) *An Invitation to Reflexive Sociology*. Polity Press.

Boysen, G.A., Kelly, T.J., Raesly, H.N. and Casner, R.W. (2014) The (mis)interpretation of teaching evaluations by college faculty and administrators. *Assessment and Evaluation in Higher Education*, 39(6), 641–656. https://doi.org/10.1080/02602938.2013.860950

REFERENCES

Bradshaw, E.L., Conigrave, J.H., Steward, B.A., Ferber, K.A., Parker, P.D. and Ryan, R.M. (2022) A meta-analysis of the dark side of the American dream: Evidence for the universal wellness costs of prioritizing extrinsic over intrinsic goals. *Journal of Personality and Social Psychology*, 124(4), 873–899. https://doi.org/10.1037/pspp0000431

Brainard, L. (2024) What is creativity? *The Philosophical Quarterly*. https://doi.org/10.1093/pq/pqae075

Brentnall, C., Rodríguez, I.D. and Culkin, N. (2018) The contribution of realist evaluation to critical analysis of the effectiveness of entrepreneurship education competitions. *Industry and Higher Education*, 32(6), 405–417. https://doi.org/10.1177/0950422218807499

Buckley, A.P. (2016) Using Contribution Analysis to evaluate small & medium enterprise support policy. *Evaluation*, 22(2), 129–148. https://doi.org/10.1177/1356389016638625

Burgin, A. (2015) *The Great Persuasion: Reinventing Free Markets since the Depression*. Harvard University Press. https://doi.org/10.4159/harvard.9780674067431

Callon, M., Lascoumes, P. and Barthe, Y. (2009) *Acting in an Uncertain World: An Essay on Technical Democracy*. The MIT Press.

Campbell, D.T. (1979) Assessing the impact of planned social change. *Evaluation and Program Planning*, 2(1), 67–90. https://doi.org/https://doi.org/10.1016/0149-7189(79)90048-X

Canina, M., Bruno, C. and Monestier, E. (2020) Futures thinking. In *The Palgrave Encyclopedia of the Possible* (pp 1–7). Springer International Publishing. https://doi.org/10.1007/978-3-319-98390-5_272-1

Chao, G.T. and Moon, H. (2005) The cultural mosaic: A metatheory for understanding the complexity of culture. *Journal of Applied Psychology*, 90(6), 1128–1140. https://doi.org/10.1037/0021-9010.90.6.1128

Chen, S.-K., Yang, Y.-T.C., Lin, C. and Lin, S.S.J. (2022) Dispositions of 21st-century skills in STEM programs and their changes over time. *International Journal of Science and Mathematics Education*. https://doi.org/10.1007/s10763-022-10288-0

Chi, M.T.H. and Wylie, R. (2014) The ICAP framework: Linking cognitive engagement to active learning outcomes. *Educational Psychologist*, 49(4), 219–243. https://doi.org/10.1080/00461520.2014.965823

Chinn, C.A., Barzilai, S. and Duncan, R.G. (2020) Education for a 'post-truth' world: New directions for research and practice. *Educational Researcher*, 50(1), 51–60. https://doi.org/10.3102/0013189x20940683

Cilesiz, S. and Greckhamer, T. (2020) Qualitative comparative analysis in education research: Its current status and future potential. *Review of Research in Education*, 44(1), 332–369. https://doi.org/10.3102/0091732x20907347

Coles, T. (2008) Finding space in the field of masculinity: Lived experiences of men's masculinities. *Journal of Sociology*, 44(3), 233–248. https://doi.org/10.1177/1440783308092882

Connell, R. (2013) The neoliberal cascade and education: An essay on the market agenda and its consequences. *Critical Studies in Education*, 54(2), 99–112. https://doi.org/10.1080/17508487.2013.776990

Dahiya, B. and Das, A. (eds) (2020) *New Urban Agenda in Asia-Pacific Governance for Sustainable and Inclusive Cities* (1st edn). Springer. https://doi.org/10.1007/978-981-13-6709-0

Darling-Hammond, L., Flook, L., Cook-Harvey, C., Barron, B. and Osher, D. (2020) Implications for educational practice of the science of learning and development. *Applied Developmental Science*, 24(2), 97–140. https://doi.org/10.1080/10888691.2018.1537791

Davies, W. (2019) *Nervous States: Democracy and the Decline of Reason* (1st edn). W.W. Norton & Company, Inc.

Deci, E.L. and Ryan, R.M. (1985) *Intrinsic Motivation and Self-Determination in Human Behavior*. Springer US. https://doi.org/10.1007/978-1-4899-2271-7

Devis, D., Fowler, S., Vieira, M., Giannoni, K., Gabriel, F., Kennedy, J., et al (2023) *From Insight to Action: Strategies for Cultivating Equity and Empowering Women in Industry*. University of South Australia. https://doi.org/10.25954/1cdy-bq37

Dewey, J. (1929) *The Quest for Certainty*. Minton, Balch.

Dishon, G. and Gilead, T. (2021) Adaptability and its discontents: 21st-century skills and the preparation for an unpredictable future. *British Journal of Educational Studies*, 69(4), 393–413. https://doi.org/10.1080/00071005.2020.1829545

Dochy, F., Segers, M., Van den Bossche, P. and Gijbels, D. (2003) Effects of problem-based learning: A meta-analysis. *Learning and Instruction*, 13(5), 533–568. https://doi.org/10.1016/s0959-4752(02)00025-7

Dunleavy, P., Margetts, H., Bastow, S. and Tinkler, J. (2006) New public management is dead: Long live digital-era governance. *Journal of Public Administration Research and Theory*, 16(3), 467–494. https://doi.org/10.1093/jopart/mui057

Efklides, A. (2011) Interactions of metacognition with motivation and affect in self-regulated learning: The MASRL model. *Educational Psychologist*, 46(1), 6–25. https://doi.org/10.1080/00461520.2011.538645

Engeström, Y. (1987) *Learning by Expanding: An Activity-theoretical Approach to Developmental Research*. Orienta-Konsultit.

Engeström, Y. (2006) Activity theory and expansive design. In S. Bagnara and G.C. Smith (eds) *Theories and Practice in Interaction Design* (pp 3–23). Lawrence Erlbaum.

Engeström, Y. and Sannino, A. (2010) Studies of expansive learning: Foundations, findings and future challenges. *Educational Research Review*, 5, 1–24.

Engeström, Y. and Sannino, A. (2021) From mediated actions to heterogenous coalitions: Four generations of activity-theoretical studies of work and learning. *Mind, Culture and Activity*, 28(1), 4–23. https://doi.org/10.1080/10749039.2020.1806328

Evans, P., Vansteenkiste, M., Parker, P., Kingsford-Smith, A. and Zhou, S. (2024) Cognitive load theory and its relationships with motivation: A self-determination theory perspective. *Educational Psychology Review*, 36(1), Article 7. https://doi.org/10.1007/s10648-023-09841-2

Feinstein, A. and Horwitz, R. (1997) Problems in the 'evidence' of 'evidence-based medicine'. *The American Journal of Medicine*, 103(6), 529–535. https://doi.org/10.1016/S0002-9343(97)00244-1

Fiorella, L. (2023) Making sense of generative learning. *Educational Psychology Review*, 35(2), Article 50. https://doi.org/10.1007/s10648-023-09769-7

Flavell, J.H. (1979) Metacognition and cognitive monitoring: A new area of cognitive-developmental inquiry. *The American Psychologist*, 34(10), 906–911. https://doi.org/10.1037/0003-066X.34.10.906

Fogle, N. and Theiner, G. (2018) The 'ontological complicity' of habitus and field: Bourdieu as an externalist. In J.A. Carter, A. Clark, J. Kallestrup, S.O. Palermos and D. Pritchard (eds) *Socially Extended Epistemology* (pp 220–252). Oxford University Press. https://doi.org/10.1093/oso/9780198801764.001.0001

Foucault, M. (2017) *Subjectivity and Truth Lectures at the Collège de France, 1980–1981* (1st edn). Palgrave Macmillan. https://doi.org/10.1007/978-1-349-73900-4

Fowler, S. and Leonard, S.N. (2021) Using design based research to shift perspectives: A model for sustainable professional development for the innovative use of digital tools. *Professional Development in Education*, 1–13. https://doi.org/10.1080/19415257.2021.1955732

Fowler, S., Cutting, C., Fiedler, S.H.D. and Leonard, S.N. (2022[[a]]) Design-based research in mathematics education: Trends, challenges and potential. *Mathematics Education Research Journal*. https://doi.org/10.1007/s13394-021-00407-5

Fowler, S., Gabriel, F. and Leonard, S.N. (2022[[b]]) Exploring the effect of teacher ontological and epistemic cognition on engagement with professional development. *Professional Development in Education*, 1–17. https://doi.org/10.1080/19415257.2022.2131600

French, M., Hesselgreaves, H., Wilson, R., Hawkins, M. and Lowe, T. (2023) *Harnessing Complexity for Better Outcomes in Public and Non-Profit Services*. Policy Press. https://doi.org/10.51952/9781447364139

Geertz, C. (1973) *The Interpretation of Cultures Selected Essays*. Basic Books.

Giddens, A. (1979) *Central Problems in Social Theory: Action, Structure and Contradiction in Social Analysis*. University of California Press.

González-Salamanca, J.C., Agudelo, O.L. and Salinas, J. (2020) Key competences, education for sustainable development and strategies for the development of 21st century skills: A systematic literature review. *Sustainability*, 12(24), Article 10366. https://www.mdpi.com/2071-1050/12/24/10366

Goodyear, P. and Markauskaite, L. (2018) Epistemic resourcefulness and the development of evaluative judgement. In D. Boud, R. Aijawi, P. Dawson and J. Tai (eds) *Developing Evaluative Judgement in Higher Education* (pp 28–38). Routledge. https://doi.org/10.4324/9781315109251

Gordon, L. and Whitty, G. (1997) Giving the 'hidden hand' a helping hand? The rhetoric and reality of neoliberal education reform in England and New Zealand. *Comparative Education*, 33(3), 453–467. https://doi.org/10.1080/03050069728460

Gorostiaga Derqui, J.M. (2001) Educational decentralization policies in Argentina and Brazil: Exploring the new trends. *Journal of Education Policy*, 16(6), 561–583. https://doi.org/10.1080/02680930110087825

Gregory, T. and Brinkman, S. (2020) *Wellbeing and Engagement Collection (WEC): History of the WEC in the South Australian School System and Psychometric Properties of the WEC Survey Instrument*. SA Department for Education and the Telethon Kids Institute. Available at: https://www.education.sa.gov.au/docs/system-performance/fraser-mustard-centre/sa-wec-technical-report.pdf

Grenfell, M.J. (2014) *Pierre Bourdieu: Key Concepts*. Routledge.

Hadwin, A., Järvelä, S. and Miller, M. (2017) Self-regulation, co-regulation, and shared regulation in collaborative learning environments. In D.H. Schunk and J. Greene (eds) *Handbook of Self-Regulation of Learning and Performance* (2nd edn, pp 83–107). Routledge.

Hall, P. (1993) Policy paradigms, social learning and the state: The case of economic policy making in Britain. *Comparative Politics*, April, 275–296.

Hargreaves, A., Crocker, R., Davis, B., McEwen, L., Sahlberg, P., Shirley, D., et al (2009) *The Learning Mosaic: A Multiple Perspective Review of the Alberta Intiative for School Improvement (AISI)*. Alberta Education.

Hattie, J. (2009) *Visible Learning: A Synthesis of Over 800 Meta-analyses Relating to Achievement*. Routledge.

Hayek, F. (1945) The use of knowledge in society. *American Economic Review*, 35(4), 27–38.

Hayek, F. (2014) *The Market and Other Orders*, edited by B. Caldwell. Routledge. https://doi.org/10.4324/9781315734866

Helgetun, J.B. and Menter, I. (2020) From an age of measurement to an evidence era? Policy-making in teacher education in England. *Journal of Education Policy*. https://doi.org/10.1080/02680939.2020.1748722

Hood, C. (1991) A public management for all seasons? *Public Administration*, 69(1), 3–19. https://doi.org/10.1111/j.1467-9299.1991.tb00779.x

Huang, J. and Sang, G. (2023) Conceptualising critical thinking and its research in teacher education: A systematic review. *Teachers and Teaching*, 1–23. https://doi.org/10.1080/13540602.2023.2212364

Hutchins, E. (2010) Cognitive ecology. *Top Cognitive Science*, 2(4), 705–715. https://doi.org/10.1111/j.1756-8765.2010.01089.x

Järvelä, S., Nguyen, A. and Hadwin, A. (2023) Human and artificial intelligence collaboration for socially shared regulation in learning. *British Journal of Educational Technology*. https://doi.org/https://doi.org/10.1111/bjet.13325

Johnson, L., Devis, D., Bacholer, C. and Leonard, S.N. (2024) Closing the loop by expanding the scope: Using learning analytics within a pragmatic adaptive engagement with complex learning environments. *Frontiers in Education*, 9. https://doi.org/10.3389/feduc.2024.1379520

Karsten, S. (1999) Neoliberal education reform in The Netherlands. *Comparative Education*, 35(3), 303–317. https://doi.org/10.1080/03050069927847

Kemmis, S. (2019) *A Practice Sensibility: An Invitation to the Theory of Practice Architectures*. Springer. https://doi.org/10.1007/978-981-32-9539-1

Kemmis, S., Wilkinson, J., Edwards-Groves, C., Hardy, I., Grootenboer, P. and Bristol, L. (2014a) *Changing Practices, Changing Education*. Springer. https://doi.org/10.1007/978-981-4560-47-4

Kemmis, S., Wilkinson, J., Edwards-Groves, C., Hardy, I., Grootenboer, P. and Bristol, L. (2014b) Student learning: Learning practices. In S. Kemmis, J. Wilkinson, C. Edwards-Groves, I. Hardy, P. Grootenboer and L. Bristol (eds) *Changing Practices, Changing Education* (pp 55–91). Springer Singapore. https://doi.org/10.1007/978-981-4560-47-4_4

Kennedy, G., Scott, W. and Campbell, A. (2020) Towards the integration of organisational culture models into model-based systems engineering approaches for enterprise systems transformation. *Australian Journal of Multi-Disciplinary Engineering*, 16(1), 80–92.

Kennedy, J., Quinn, F. and Taylor, N. (2016) The school science attitude survey: A new instrument for measuring attitudes towards school science. *International Journal of Research & Method in Education*, 39(4), 422–445. https://doi.org/10.1080/1743727x.2016.1160046

King, R.B., Haw, J.Y. and Wang, Y. (2024) Need-support facilitates well-being across cultural, economic, and political contexts: A self-determination theory perspective. *Learning and Instruction*, 93, Article 101978. https://doi.org/https://doi.org/10.1016/j.learninstruc.2024.101978

Kopycinski, P. and Mazur, S. (2017) *Public Policy and the Neo-Weberian State*. Routledge.

Latour, B. (2005) *Reassembling the Social: An Introduction to Actor-network-Theory*. Oxford University Press.

Lemire, S., Bohni Nielsen, S. and Dybdal, L. (2012) Making contribution analysis work: A practical framework for handling influencing factors and alternative explanations. *Evaluation*, 18, 294–309. https://doi.org/10.1177/1356389012450654

León, J. and Núñez, J.L. (2013) Causal ordering of basic psychological needs and well-being. *Social Indicators Research*, 114(2), 243–253. https://doi.org/10.1007/s11205-012-0143-4

Li, I.W. and Carroll, D.R. (2020) Factors influencing dropout and academic performance: An Australian higher education equity perspective. *Journal of Higher Education Policy and Management*, 42(1), 14–30.

Lingard, B. (2020) Toward a global political sociology of school choice policies. *Educational Policy*, 34(1), 261–280. https://doi.org/10.1177/0895904819888233

Lingard, B., Sellar, S. and Baroutsis, A. (2015) Researching the habitus of global policy actors in education. *Cambridge Journal of Education*, 45(1), 25–42. https://doi.org/10.1080/0305764X.2014.988686

Lohmeyer, B.A. and Taylor, N. (2021) War, heroes and sacrifice: Masking neoliberal violence during the COVID-19 pandemic. *Critical Sociology*, 47(4–5), 625–639. https://doi.org/10.1177/0896920520975824

Lowrie, T. and Jorgensen, R. (2012) Teaching mathematics remotely: Changed practices in distance education. *Mathematics Education Research Journal*, 24(3), 371–383. https://doi.org/10.1007/s13394-011-0031-2

Lupton, R. and Hayes, D. (2021) *Great Mistakes in Education Policy: And How to Avoid Them in the Future* (1st edn). Policy Press. https://doi.org/10.46692/9781447352464

Mahon, K., Kemmis, S., Francisco, S. and Lloyd, A. (2017) Introduction: Practice theory and the theory of practice architectures. In K. Mahon, S. Francisco and S. Kemmis (eds) *Exploring Education and Professional Practice: Through the Lens of Practice Architectures* (pp 1–30). Springer. https://doi.org/10.1007/978-981-10-2219-7_1

Mayne, J. (2008) Contribution analysis: An approach to exploring cause and effect. *ILAC Briefs*, 16.

Mayne, J. (2011) Contribution analysis: Addressing cause and effect. In R. Schwartz, K. Forss and M. Marra (eds) *Evaluating the Complex* (pp 53–96). Transaction Publishers.

Mayne, J. (2012) Contribution analysis: Coming of age? *Evaluation*, 18, 270–280. https://doi.org/10.1177/1356389012451663

McKenney, S. and Reeves, T.C. (2013) *Conducting Educational Design Research*. Taylor & Francis. https://doi.org/10.4324/9780203818183

Mengel, F., Sauermann, J. and Zölitz, U. (2019) Gender bias in teaching evaluations. *Journal of the European Economic Association*, 17(2), 535–566. https://doi.org/10.1093/jeea/jvx057

Metcalfe, J. (2017) Learning from errors. *Annual Review of Psychology*, 68, 465–489. https://doi.org/https://doi.org/10.1146/annurev-psych-010416-044022

Ministers' Media Centre (2023) Major reform to improve teacher training and better prepare teachers for the classroom [Press release]. Australian Government. Available at: https://ministers.education.gov.au/clare/major-reform-improve-teacher-training-and-better-prepare-teachers-classroom#:~:text="Teachers%20have%20the%20biggest%20impact,teaching%20practices%20which%20work%20best

Mirowski, P. and Plehwe, D. (eds) (2015) *The Road from Mont Pelerin: The Making of the Neoliberal Thought Collective*. Harvard University Press. https://doi.org/10.4159/9780674054264

Morgan, D.F. and Cook, B.J. (eds) (2015) *New Public Governance: A Regime-centered Perspective*. Routledge. https://doi.org/10.4324/9781315702100

Morowitz, H.J. (1994) *The Mind, the Brain and Complex Adaptive Systems*. Routledge. https://doi.org/https://doi.org/10.4324/9780429492761

Murphy, M. and Costa, C. (2015) *Theory as Method in Research: On Bourdieu, Social Theory and Education* (1st edn). Routledge. https://doi.org/10.4324/9781315707303

Musso, M., Kyndt, E., Cascallar, E. and Dochy, F. (2012) Predicting mathematical performance: The effect of cognitive processes and self-regulation factors. *Education Research International*, 1–13. https://doi.org/10.1155/2012/250719

National Research Council (2012) *Education for Life and Work: Developing Transferable Knowledge and Skills in the 21st Century*. The National Academies Press. https://doi.org/doi:10.17226/13398

OECD (2020) *The OECD Learning Compass*. Available at: https://www.oecd.org/en/data/tools/oecd-learning-compass-2030.html

Osborne, S.P., Radnor, Z. and Nasi, G. (2013) A new theory for public service management? Toward a (public) service-dominant approach. *American Review of Public Administration*, 43(2), 135–158. https://doi.org/10.1177/0275074012466935

Panadero, E. (2017) A review of self-regulated learning: Six models and four directions for research. *Frontiers in Psychology*, 8, Article 422. https://doi.org/10.3389/fpsyg.2017.00422

Panadero, E. and Alonso-Tapia, J. (2014) How do students self-regulate? Review of Zimmerman's cyclical model of self-regulated learning. *Anales de psicologia*, 30(2), 450–462.

Partnership for 21st Century Learning (2015) *The Partnership for 21st Century Learning*. Available at: https://www.battelleforkids.org/wp-content/uploads/2023/11/P21_Framework_Definitions_New_Logo_2015_9pgs.pdf

Patton, M.Q. (2011) *Developmental Evaluation: Applying Complexity Concepts to Enhance Innovation and Use*. Guilford Press.

Patton, M.Q. (2012) A utilization-focused approach to contribution analysis. *Evaluation*, 18(3), 364–377.

Patton, M.Q. (2015) Book review: Evaluating the complex: Attribution, contribution, and beyond. *American Journal of Evaluation*, 36(3), 419–429. https://doi.org/10.1177/1098214015569758

Peck, F.A., Renga, I.P., Wu, K. and Erickson, D. (2021) The durability and invisibility of practice fields: Insights from math teachers doing math. *Cognition and Instruction*, 1–28. https://doi.org/10.1080/07370008.2021.1983577

Perrotta, C. and Williamson, B. (2018) The social life of Learning Analytics: Cluster analysis and the 'performance' of algorithmic education. *Learning, Media and Technology*, 43(1), 3–16. https://doi.org/10.1080/17439884.2016.1182927

Perry, K.E., Donohue, K.M. and Weinstein, R.S. (2007) Teaching practices and the promotion of achievement and adjustment in first grade. *Journal of School Psychology*, 45(3), 269–292. https://doi.org/https://doi.org/10.1016/j.jsp.2007.02.005

Plucker, J.A. and Beghetto, R.A. (2004) Why creativity is domain general, why it looks domain specific, and why the distinction does not matter. In R.J. Sternberg (ed) *Handbook of Creativity* (pp 153–167). American Psychological Association. https://doi.org/10.1037/10692-009

Pollitt, C. and Bouckaert, G. (2011) *Public Management Reform a Comparative Analysis: New Public Management, Governance, and the Neo-Weberian State* (3rd edn). Oxford University Press.

Productivity Commission (2016) *National Education Evidence Base: Draft Report*. Productivity Commission.

Puryear, J.S. and Lamb, K.N. (2020) Defining creativity: How far have we come since Plucker, Beghetto, and Dow? *Creativity Research Journal*, 32(3), 206–214. https://doi.org/10.1080/10400419.2020.1821552

Reeve, J. and Cheon, S.H. (2024) Learning how to become an autonomy-supportive teacher begins with perspective taking: A randomized control trial and model test. *Teaching and Teacher Education*, 148, Article 104702. https://doi.org/https://doi.org/10.1016/j.tate.2024.104702

Rogers, T. (2015) *Critical Realism and Learning Analytics Research: Epistemological Implications of an Ontological Foundation*. Proceedings of the Fifth International Conference on Learning Analytics and Knowledge, Poughkeepsie, New York. https://doi-org.access.library.unisa.edu.au/10.1145/2723576.2723631

Roth, W.-M. and Lee, Y.-J. (2007) 'Vygotsky's neglected legacy': Cultural-historical activity theory. *Review of Educational Research*, 77(2), 186–232. https://doi.org/10.3102/0034654306298273

Rowe, E., Lubienski, C., Skourdoumbis, A., Gerrard, J. and Hursh, D. (2019) Exploring alternatives to the 'neoliberalism' critique: New language for contemporary global reform. *Discourse*, 40(2), 147–149. https://doi.org/10.1080/01596306.2019.1579409

Rowlands, J. and Rawolle, S. (2013) Neoliberalism is not a theory of everything: A Bourdieuian analysis of illusio in educational research. *Critical Studies in Education*, 54(3), 260–272. https://doi.org/10.1080/17508487.2013.830631

Ryan, R.M. and Deci, E.L. (2020) Intrinsic and extrinsic motivation from a self-determination theory perspective: Definitions, theory, practices, and future directions. *Contemporary Educational Psychology*, 61, 101860. https://doi.org/10.1016/j.cedpsych.2020.101860

Sandoval, W. (2014) Conjecture mapping: An approach to systematic educational design research. *Journal of the Learning Sciences*, 23(1), 18–36. https://doi.org/10.1080/10508406.2013.778204

Sannino, A., Engeström, Y. and Lemos, M. (2016) Formative interventions for expansive learning and transformative agency. *Journal of the Learning Sciences*, 25(4), 599–633. https://doi.org/10.1080/10508406.2016.1204547

Schatzki, T.R. (1996) *Social Practices: A Wittgensteinian Approach to Human Activity and the Social*. Cambridge University Press.

Schatzki, T.R. (2019) *Social Change in a Material World: How Activity and Material Processes Dynamize Practices*. Routledge.

Schunk, D.H. (2020) *Learning Theories: An Educational Perspective* (8th edn). Pearson.

Schunk, D.H. and Greene, J.A. (2017) Historical, contemporary, and future perspectives on self-regulated learning and performance. In D.H. Schunk and J.A. Greene (eds) *Handbook of Self-regulation of Learning and Performance* (pp 1–15). Routledge.

Schwartz, D.L. (2024) Achieving an adaptive learner. *Educational Psychologist*, 1–16. https://doi.org/10.1080/00461520.2024.2397389

Scott, C.L. (2015) *The Futures of Learning 2: What Kind of Learning for the 21st Century?* UNESCO Education Research and Foresight. https://hdl.handle.net/20.500.12799/3709

Sellar, S. and Gulson, K.N. (2019) Becoming information centric: The emergence of new cognitive infrastructures in education policy. *Journal of Education Policy*, 1–18. https://doi.org/10.1080/02680939.2019.1678766

Singh, C.A. and Muis, K.R. (2024) An integrated model of socially shared regulation of learning: The role of metacognition, affect, and motivation. *Educational Psychologist*, 1–18. https://doi.org/10.1080/00461520.2023.2294881

Snowden, D. (2005) Strategy in the context of uncertainty. *Handbook of Business Strategy*, 6(1), 47–54. https://doi.org/10.1108/08944310510556955

Snowden, D. (2012) The social ecology of knowledge management. In *Knowledge Horizons: The Present and the Promise of Knowledge Management* (pp 237–266). Routledge. https://doi.org/10.4324/9780080496016

Spinuzzi, C. and Guile, D. (2019) Fourth-generation activity theory: An integrative literature review and implications for professional communication. In *2019 IEEE International Professional Communication Conference (ProComm)* (pp 37–45). IEEE.

Stacey, R.D. (2007) *Strategic Management and Organisational Dynamics: The Challenge of Complexity to Ways of Thinking about Organisations*. Prentice Hall.

Steuer, G., Tulis, M. and Peterson, E.R. (2024) Learning from errors and failure in educational contexts. *British Journal of Educational Psychology*. https://doi.org/10.1111/bjep.12723

Stiglbauer, B., Gnambs, T., Gamsjäger, M. and Batinic, B. (2013) The upward spiral of adolescents' positive school experiences and happiness: Investigating reciprocal effects over time. *Journal of School Psychology*, 51(2), 231–242. https://doi.org/10.1016/j.jsp.2012.12.002

Svihla, V. (2010) Collaboration as a dimension of design innovation. *CoDesign: Creativity and Cognition*, 6(4), 245–262. https://doi.org/10.1080/15710882.2010.533186

Sweller, J. (1994) Cognitive load theory, learning difficulty, and instructional design. *Learning and Instruction*, 4(4), 295–312.

Taylor, G., Jungert, T., Mageau, G.A., Schattke, K., Dedic, H., Rosenfield, S., et al (2014) A self-determination theory approach to predicting school achievement over time: The unique role of intrinsic motivation. *Contemporary Educational Psychology*, 39(4), 342–358. https://doi.org/10.1016/j.cedpsych.2014.08.002

Tett, L. and Hamilton, M. (2019) *Resisting Neoliberalism in Education: Local, National and Transnational Perspectives*. Policy Press. https://doi.org/10.56687/9781447350064

Tomasello, M. (2016) The ontogeny of cultural learning. *Current Opinion in Psychology*, 8, 1–4.

Trilling, B. and Fadel, C. (2009) *21st Century Skills: Learning for Life in Our Times* (1st edn). Wiley.

Tronco, T.R. (2010) A brief history of the internet. In T. Tronco (ed) *New Network Architectures: The Path to the Future Internet* (pp 1–11). Springer. https://doi.org/10.1007/978-3-642-13247-6_1

Uhl-Bien, M., Marion, R. and McKelvey, B. (2007) Complexity leadership theory: Shifting leadership from the industrial age to the knowledge era. *The Leadership Quarterly*, 18(4), 298–318.

UNDP Global Centre for Public Service Excellence (2018) *Foresight Manual: Empowered Futures for the 2030 Agenda*. UNDP Global Centre for Public Service Excellence. Available at: https://www.undp.org/sites/g/files/zskgke326/files/publications/UNDP_ForesightManual_2018.pdf

Uttl, B., White, C.A. and Gonzalez, D.W. (2017) Meta-analysis of faculty's teaching effectiveness: Student evaluation of teaching ratings and student learning are not related. *Studies in Educational Evaluation*, 54, 22–42. https://doi.org/10.1016/j.stueduc.2016.08.007

Veale, M. and Brass, I. (2019) *Administration by Algorithm? Public Management Meets Public Sector Machine Learning*. Oxford University Press. https://doi.org/10.1093/oso/9780198838494.003.0006

Vieira, M., Kennedy, J., Leonard, S.N. and Cropley, D. (2024) Creative self-efficacy: Why it matters for the future of STEM education. *Creativity Research Journal*, 1–17. https://doi.org/10.1080/10400419.2024.2309038

Vygotsky, L.S., Cole, M., John-Steiner, V., Scribner, S. and Souberman, E. (1978) *Mind in Society: Development of Higher Psychological Processes* (1st edn). Harvard University Press.

Wilkins, A., Collet-Sabé, J., Gobby, B. and Hangartner, J. (2019) Translations of new public management: A decentred approach to school governance in four OECD countries. *Globalisation, Societies and Education*, 17(2), 147–160. https://doi.org/10.1080/14767724.2019.1588102

Williamson, B. and Piattoeva, N. (2019) Objectivity as standardization in data-scientific education policy, technology and governance. *Learning, Media and Technology: The Datafication of Education*, 44(1), 64–76. https://doi.org/10.1080/17439884.2018.1556215

REFERENCES

Winne, P.H. (2022) Modeling self-regulated learning as learners doing learning science: How trace data and learning analytics help develop skills for self-regulated learning. *Metacognition and Learning*, 17(3), 773–791. https://doi.org/10.1007/s11409-022-09305-y

Woolcott, G., Keast, R. and Pickernell, D. (2019) Deep impact: Reconceptualising university research impact using human cultural accumulation theory. *Studies in Higher Education*, 45(6), 1–20. https://doi.org/10.1080/03075079.2019.1594179

Woolcott, G., Leonard, S., Scott, A., Keast, R. and Chamberlain, D. (2021) Partnered research and emergent variation: Developing a set of characteristics for identifying complexity in higher education partnerships. *Journal of Higher Education Policy and Management*, 43(1), 91–109. https://doi.org/10.1080/1360080X.2020.1733734

World Economic Forum (2015) *New Vision for Education: Fostering Social and Emotional Learning through Technology*. Available at: https://www3.weforum.org/docs/WEF_New_Vision_for_Education.pdf

Yamagata-Lynch, L.C. (2010) *Activity Systems Analysis Methods: Understanding Complex Learning Environments*. Springer.

Yu, J., Kreijkes, P. and Salmela-Aro, K. (2023) Interconnected trajectories of achievement goals, academic achievement, and well-being: Insights from an expanded goal framework. *Learning and Individual Differences*, 108, Article 102384. https://doi.org/https://doi.org/10.1016/j.lindif.2023.102384

Zedelius, C.M. and Schooler, J.W. (2015) Mind wandering 'ahas' versus mindful reasoning: Alternative routes to creative solutions. *Frontiers in Psychology*, 6, 834–834. https://doi.org/10.3389/fpsyg.2015.00834

Zheng, J., Lajoie, S. and Li, S. (2023) Emotions in self-regulated learning: A critical literature review and meta-analysis. *Frontiers in Psychology*, 14, Article 1137010. https://doi.org/10.3389/fpsyg.2023.1137010

Zimmerman, B.J. (1989) A social cognitive view of self-regulated academic learning. *Journal of Educational Psychology*, 81(3), 329–339. https://doi.org/10.1037/0022-0663.81.3.329

Zimmerman, B.J. (2000) Attaining self-regulation: A social cognitive perspective. In M. Boekaerts, M. Zeidner and P.R. Pintrich (eds) *Handbook of Self-regulation* (pp 13–39). Elsevier.

Zolfaghari, B., Möllering, G., Clark, T. and Dietz, G. (2016) How do we adopt multiple cultural identities? A multidimensional operationalization of the sources of culture. *European Management Journal*, 34(2), 102–113. https://doi.org/https://doi.org/10.1016/j.emj.2016.01.003

Index

References to figures appear in *italic* type; those in **bold** type refer to tables.

3GAT (third generation Activity Theory) 11, 13, 40, 146, 148
4Cs (Communication, Collaboration, Creativity and Critical Thinking) 42, 44, 45–46, 48, 148
4GAT (fourth generation Activity Theory) 9, 148
21st-century skills 42, **52**, 148

A

Aboriginal education 36
actionable knowledge, grounded 141
activity system model 133
Activity Systems Analysis 11, 40, 83, 146
Activity Theory (AT) 3, 11–13, 50, 70, 72, 122, 129
  definition 148
  3GAT 11, 13, 40, 140, 146, 148
  4GAT 9, 148
Actor Network Theory 22
adaptive agents 77
adaptive leadership
  definition 6, 148
  and enabling leadership 7
administrative leadership 6, 7, 149
affect 58
Australian Productivity Commission 26
autonomy 60, 61, 114

B

balancing feedback loop 110
Bandura, Albert 55
Biesta, G. 21
Boekaerts, M. 55, 57, 130
boundary-spanning 121
Bourdieu, Pierre 19, 21, 31, 40, 65–66

C

Callon et al 20, 33
capital (Bourdieu) 65, 149
CFC (Corroboree Frog College), contextualising 95–96
change, theory of *see* Theory of Change (ToC)
Cilesiz, S. 24
classroom learning system 74–75, **74**
cognitive engagement 105, *106*, 107, *108*
Cognitive Load Theory 57, 149
collaboration 43–44, 46, **52**
communication 43, 46, **52**
Communities of Practice (CoP) 72, 85, 149
community (activity theory concept) 75, 129, 149
competence 60–61
complex adaptive systems 77–78
complexity 4–6, 77, 116–117

Complexity Leadership Theory
  (CLT) 2, 6, 8
  definition 149
complexity theory 37, 122, 146
complexity thinking 117
complex problems 72, 73, 77, 154
complex school site 144
composite score 101
conceptual understanding 13, 49,
  53, 98, 112, 136, 137
  and feedback loops 108
  and tension 111, 113
conjecture mapping 11
connectedness to school *106, 108*
Contribution Analysis (CA)
  35–36
Contribution Analysis (Mayne) 2
control beliefs 57, 58
creative thinking 45
creativity 44, 46, **52**
critical thinking 45, 46, **52**
cultural capital 65, 66
cultural-discursive practice
  architectures 67
Cultural-Historical Activity
  Theory (CHAT) 70, 72, 149
cultural historical theory 22

D

Darling-Hammond et al 49, 50
Davies, W. 24
Deci, E.L. 60
deep thinking 68–69
design-based learning 45
Design-Based Research
  (DBR) 14–15, 83, 132, 142
  definition 149–150
design evaluation protocol *139*
Design Thinking 10–11, **12**, 15,
  96, 137–138, 145
  definition 132, 150
Developmental Evaluation
  (Patton) 2
Dewey, J. 37
diversity, equity and inclusion
  (DEI) 144–145
Dochy et al 28
doxa 23

E

Educational Design
  Research 14–15
educational reform 40–41
effort 57, 58, 59, 111, 130
Efklides, A. 57–58
emotional development 50, **52**
emotion regulation 105–106,
  106, 108
emotions 55, 57
enablers 96, 110, 114, 116, 124, 138
  and *Professional Certificate in
    Futures Oriented Learning* 118
  and sheep shearing 86–87,
    90, 94
enabling leadership 6–7, 150
Engeström, Y. 9, 40, 70, 146, 148
epistemic fluency 140–141, 150
evaluation 137, 138–140, 144
Expansive Learning Theory 2,
  146, 150
extrinsic motivation 59–60

F

feedback loops 108, 110–111, 114
Feinstein, A. 26–27
fetishism 19
field, definition 150
field theory 40, 65–66
Foucault, M. 24
Futures Modelling 10, **12**, 14, 91–93
  definition 150
Futures Thinking 10, 11, **12**,
  133, 135
  definition 150

G

game analogy, Bourdieu 31
generative artificial
  intelligence 45, 151
Greckhamer, T. 24
Gulson, K.N. 23, 29–30

H

habitus 65–66, 69, 151
Hall, P.A. 24

Hattie, J. 27
Hayek, F. 19–20, 26, 27, 32, 33, 34, 37
Horwitz, R. 26–27

I

illusio 19, 26, 30, 31, 151
informal networks 121
information-sharing architectures 23
intrinsic motivation 59, 60

K

Kemmis, Stephen 21, 66–67
knowledge problem 19–20, 26, 33, 34

L

labour, division of 85, 115, 146
leadership, types 6–8
learning activity system 98, *99*, 104, 105, *109*, *119*
Learning Analytics 121
learning-to-learn skills 49
'life after school' 40

M

macro-system 129–132
macrotensions 126
mass education 22, 29, 41
material-economic practices 67, 68, 69
metacognition 55, 58, 151
'Metacognition and Affect in Self-Regulated Learning' (MASRL) model 57–58
metacognitive instruction 50
metacognitive learning 131
metacognitive regulation 57
Mont Pelerin Society 38
motivation 57, 58, 59–61, 115, 130
Musso et al 28

N

NAPLAN 41
neoliberal education 111–112

neoliberalism 18, 19, 25–26, 31, 32, 37
  definition 1–2, 151
Neo-Weberian State (NWS) 32, 33–34, 151
networks 121
New Public Governance (NPG) 21, 32–33, 151
New Public Management (NPM) 18, 19, 22–25, 31, 32
  definition 151
  and NWS 33–34

O

objective 22, 23, 26, 113, 124
  definition 152
object of transformation 12, 69, 74, 75, 83, 97
  definition 152
  and complexity thinking 117
  and conceptual understanding 98
  and PAM 94
  and SRL 135
  and STEM 145
Organization for Economic Co-operation and Development (OECD) 46, *47*, 48
  transformative competencies 53, 152
outcome 6, 13, 30, 34, 50, 57
  definition 152
  and assumption 81
  and change to activity systems 102
  complex 126
  describes a system behaviour 135
  and educated citizen 41
  and enablers 110
  and feedback loop 114
  and Futures Modelling 91
  huge number of variables affecting 73
  and object of transformation 69
  and *Professional Certificate in Futures Oriented Learning* 120
  and risks 136
  and sheep shearing 80, 93
  in the SoLD model 51, 53

and SRL 54
and tensions 111, 113
and Theory of Change 138

P

parallel activity 11, **92**, 148, 152
Partnership for 21st Century Learning 42
Piattoeva, N. 23–24
practice architectures 21, 66–70, 152
practice theories 64–67, 152
Pragmatic Adaptive Design (PAD) 11, 123, 124, 132–133, 138, 142
  definition 152
Pragmatic Adaptive Leadership (PAL)
  definition 152
  practices 9–15
Pragmatic Adaptive Modelling (PAM) 10, 63, 78–79, 120, 123, 124, 125, 126, *127*, 129
  definition 152
  describes the mechanisms and processes of learning 143–144
  and Design Thinking 138
  framework for meaningful change 122
  and researcher data 140
  and Research-Informed Design 135
  and STEM 145
  and systems modelling 94
  theory 8–9
  woolly example 79–91
pragmatic adaptive policy making 36–38
problem-based learning (PBL) 28, 45
problem solving 45, 69
  see also Design Thinking
productive instructional strategies 49–50, **52**
Professional Certificate in Futures Oriented Learning 118–119, 120
project-based learning 45

R

randomised control trial (RCT) 26–27, 35
  definition 153
Rawolle, S. 19, 21
Reflexive Practice 10–11, 132
Reflexive Review **12**, 15, 141–142, 153
reflexivity, definition 141
reinforcing feedback loop 110–111
relatedness, and intrinsic motivation 61
relatings practices 66, 70
Research-Informed Design 10–11, **12**, 15, 132, 133–142
  definition 153
responsibility, taking 46, **52**
roles 6–7, 84–85, 94, 101, 114, 126
  definition 153
Rosenthal, Ted 55
Rowlands, J. 19, 21
rules (Activity Theory concept) 72, 73, 75, 94, 101, 108
  definition 153
  and feedback loop 114
  and sheep shearing 85
Ryan, R.M. 60

S

Sandoval, W. 11
sayings practices 66, 70
School Attitudes Survey (SAS) 138, 153
school site, complex 144
Science, Technology, Engineering and Mathematics (STEM), and equity and inclusion for women 145
Science of Learning and Development (Darling-Hammond et al) 3
Science of Learning and Development (SoLD) 49–51, **52**, 53, 153
self-concept 57, 58
Self-Determination Theory (SDT) 59–61

INDEX

self-efficacy 101, 102, 115
self-regulated learning (SRL) 53–59, 60, 115, 124–126, 130, *131*, 135
 definition 154
 and social learning 133
 and tools 108
Sellar, S. 23, 29–30
sensemaking, and Snowden 77
sheep shearing 79–91, *92*, 93, 94
simultaneous activity 74, *109*, 126, 153
Situational Analysis 85–86
situational maps 40
Situation Mapping 10, 11–13, **12**, 62, 83–86
 definition 154
 and tensions 90
Snowden, D. 77
social and emotional development 50, **52**
social capital 65, 66
social learning 24, 118, 119, 120, 140, 150
 and Design Thinking 145
 and SRL 133
socio-material assemblages 21–22
socio-political arrangements 67
socio-political practice architectures 68
socio-technical infrastructure 30
strategic knowledge, transferable 50
stress 125, 130
Student Attitude Survey (SAS) 100–102, *103*, 104
students
 contextualising 97
 learning activity system 98, *99*, 104, *109*
 Student Attitude Survey (SAS) 100–104
 Wellbeing and Engagement Collection (WEC) survey 104–107
subjects (Activity Theory concept) 73, 94, 96, 117
 definition 154

summative assessment 113, 114
supersystems 76
supportive environments 49, **52**
supports, system of 50–51, **52**
symbolic capital 65
system, definition 154
systemic inertia 110
systemic resilience 110
system maps 75–76, 79
systems theory 73–78
systems thinking 73, 79, 122, 154

T

technical democracy 20
tension modelling 87–91
tensions 111–114, 117–118, 130–131
 and dilemmas, reconciling 46, **52**
Theory of Change (ToC) 96, 98, 100, 108, 136, 138
 definition 154
 and CA 35
 and sheep shearing 80, 81
 and tensions and enablers 114
thick descriptions 29
'thriving after school' challenge 16
tools 94, 97, 101, 126, 136
 definition 154
 and enablers 86
 and Reflexive Practice 132
 related to self-regulated learning 108
 and sheep shearing 83, 85
transferable strategic knowledge 50
transformation, object of *see* object of transformation
transformative competencies 46, 47, **52**

U

Uhl-Bien et al 2, 6, 122
United Nations Educational, Scientific and Cultural Organization, and 4Cs 42
US National Research Council, and 4Cs 42

V

value, creating new 46, **52**

W

Wacquant, L.J.D. 19
Wellbeing and Engagement Collection (WEC) survey 104–108, 154
wicked problems 72, 77, 141, 154
Williamson, B. 23–24

women, equity and inclusion for in STEM 145
wool 80–91, 94
World Economic Forum, and 4Cs 42
worries *106, 108*

Y

Yamagata-Lynch, L.C. 11

Z

Zimmerman, B.J. 54–55, 130